SOVIET STORM
WORLD WAR
II
ON THE RUSSIAN FRONT
1941-1945

WRITTEN BY
MIKE LEPINE

Danann
BOOKS

Danann
BOOKS

© Danann Publishing Ltd 2016

First Published Danann Publishing Ltd 2016

WARNING: For private domestic use only, any unauthorised Copying,
hiring, lending or public performance of this book set is illegal.

CAT NO: DAN0313
Photography courtesy of Getty images:

Print Collector	TASS	Galerie Bilderwelt
Laski Diffusion	Keystone	STF/AFP
ullstein bild	Fine Art Images/Heritage Images	Keystone/Hulton Archive
Photo12/UIG	LAPI/Roger Viollet	Leonard Mccombe/The LIFE Images Collection
Universal History Archive/UIG	Mondadori Portfolio	PhotoQuest
Heinrich Hoffmann/Mondadori Portfolio	Bettmann	Slava Katamidze Collection
Sovfoto/UIG	Mansell/Mansell/The LIFE Picture	Eliot Elisofon/The LIFE Picture Collection

Other images courtesy of Wiki Commons

Book layout & design Darren Grice at **Ctrl-d**
Copy Editor Tom O'Neill

Quality of original archive material may vary throughout the programme. DVD's are engineered
to the highest possible standards. Viewing experience will vary from player to player.

The owner of the copyright hereunder has licensed the material contained in the
videogram for non commercial private use only and prohibits any other use,
copying or reproduction in whole or part. This book set range is unauthorised and
is an unofficial product and are in no way affiliated with their respective clubs.
This is an independent product and is not represented as official merchandise.

All rights reserved. No Part of this title may be reproduced or transmitted in any material form (including
photocopying or storing it in any medium by electronic means and whether or not transiently or incidentally
to some other use of this publication) without the written permission of the copyright owner, except in ac-
cordance with the provisions of the Copyright, Designs and Patents Act 1988.Applications for the copyright
owner's written permission should be addressed to the publisher.

Made in EU.
ISBN: 978-0-9931813-1-3

CONTENTS

FOREWORD

GO WEST, YOUNG ADOLF

When he was just a young boy, Adolf Hitler became quite obsessed with reading Westerns. He'd devour them in his bedroom, one after the other, struggling long after dark to read by moonlight with the aid of a magnifying glass. He barely slept and his school grades slipped badly. Something had him spellbound. Something called to him from the epic tales of heroic white European settlers forging a mighty new nation out of the wilderness. Westward went the wagons and with them went true civilisation. Savage, bestial 'Injuns' were soundly defeated and put in their place in special camps or reservations. Inferior Mexicans with their stupid-looking hats and craven, backstabbing ways would be driven out of California and the South-Western territories back to where they belonged south of the Rio Grande. A new nation would rise, proud and clean, stretching from the breakers of the Atlantic to the rollers of the Pacific. One empire, one people. Ein reich, ein volk. It all seemed…very right to the young Adolf.

STALIN THE GUNSLINGER

Josef Stalin too was an aficionado of Westerns, albeit that he preferred movies. In his capacity as the great Soviet dictator, he would often hold special cinema showings for his favoured elite. He adored the films of John Ford and seemed to identify with the lone cowboy as exemplified by John Wayne. Being a world-class coward, a lonely Georgian in a world of Russians, standing only five feet four in his stockinged feet, violently pock-marked with smallpox scars and having an unnaturally short left arm, some have suggested he was desperate to enjoy the fantasy of being a real man. The Big Hombre with Colt six-guns that did all the talking he needed. The fantasy took hold. In the last year of his life, Stalin sent a team of assassins to the United States especially to kill John Wayne. In Stalin's addled mind, this town really wasn't big enough for the both of them…

MANIFEST DESTINY

The American West that so engrossed both Hitler and Stalin was forged from what — today — would seem to be a strange, almost supernatural philosophy — an ideology called Manifest Destiny. Promoted mostly by Democratic politicians, it held that it was both the American settler's destiny and duty to sweep West across the land and to forge from it something truly special. There were early echoes of 'American Exceptionalism' in all of this of course, and of darker philosophies too. There were only some 400,000 Stone Age Native Americans standing in the way and it was right and proper to push them aside and bring them to heel to deliver unto them the Protestant Work Ethic and Christianity. Mexicans were not of the same people and America could never be a single entity until their ownership, identity and influence was cast aside too. God rode with the wagon trains and smiled on those who took their responsibility of building America to heart. Slavery was fine, as Blacks weren't fully human and could provide a useful labour force to help forge the new world. At the end of the mighty endeavour would stand a nation that would provide a shining beacon to all humanity, a *'New Jerusalem'*. It's best left to individual opinion as to whether such a lofty goal was ever really achieved.

And then the Germans got hold of the idea. A German geographer called Friedrich Ratzel turned up in America in 1873 and thought that Manifest Destiny was an idea well worth exporting back home. For him, it meant Germany expanding and building an empire both in Africa and Asia. These godless benighted places could be useful for the expansion of Western — and in particular German - civilisation. It never occurred to Ratzel that the principal of Manifest Destiny could be applied within Europe itself. That idea was left to others who came later. Others like the Nazis.

LEBENSRAUM

'There's only one duty: to Germanize this country (Russia) by the immigration of Germans, and to look upon the natives as Redskins'

Adolf Hitler

The Adolf Hitler who had so adored Western stories as a child certainly took to the idea of Manifest Destiny with great enthusiasm as he developed his own political philosophy. He was inspired by those heroic settlers and pioneers and Injun-hunters. One day, he swore, the German people - like the white nation builders of the West -, would set off and build themselves a vastly expanded new nation. They would win for themselves Lebensraum (Literally, *'Living Space'*) so that the mighty Aryan Herrenvolk (*'master race'*), could achieve their true destiny. Only this time, instead of heading West, the settlers would head East across Europe and into Russia.

It didn't matter that the vast swathe of Eastern Europe that Hitler desired had people already living in it. They mattered no more than the Sioux, the Apache, the Blackfeet, the Crow or the Cheyenne. They were just Slavs and Jews. The Slavs, in Hitler's mind were bestial and subhuman (Untermenschen), racially inferior, ugly, stupid, lazy and worthless. The Jews were worse. Hitler of course subscribed to every hateful anti-Semitic stereotype but he also believed that the Jews were by their very nature Bolsheviks too — and secretly commanded the communist Soviet Union, lording it over the Slavs who were too mentally ill-equipped to ever rule themselves.

Hitler added further self-justification to his invasion plans by reasoning that, if he did not act, the West would one day be overrun both by Communism and a tidal wave of Slavs. They were, he infamously said, *'an inferior race that breed like vermin'*. Lebensraum was no more than self-defence

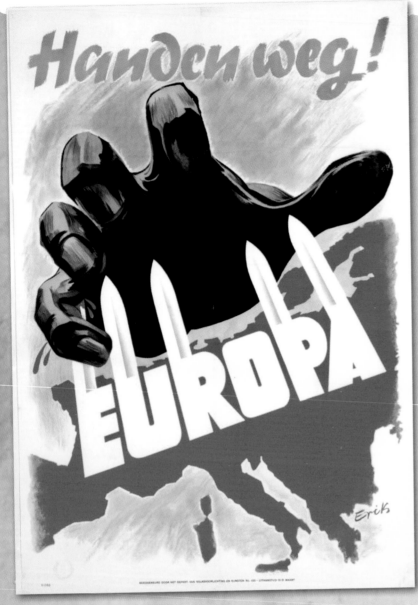

should he feel charitable — allow the survivors to scratch out an existence in the vast frigid forests and stinking swamps of Siberia. The fittest might be captured and used as slaves.

These ideas — when presented to them — did not greatly trouble the German military. Hitler was honest with them about the kind of war he envisaged and they would work — from the lowest to the highest ranks — to deliver it to him. They understood his vision and — to a degree they would later be desperate to deny — they shared his prejudices about the enemy. In other words, they understood why they needed to be exterminated. Hitler tried to reassure those few who still doubted by telling them that *'there is no such thing as a crime on the part of the Germans'*. The Germans would, he assured them, be the ones wearing the white hats when the panzers rolled…

LETS BE FRIENDS

Either Josef Stalin was just not paying attention or he was stupid. Historical opinion varies. Hitler had written in Mein Kampf in 1924:
'We are putting an end to the perpetual German march towards the south and west of Europe and turning our eyes towards the east…we must principally bear in mind Russia and the border states subject to her.'

At the 1937 Nuremberg Rally, he had explicitly referred to Russia as *'…the greatest danger for the culture and civilisation of mankind which has ever threatened it…'*

The Führer had even told League of Nations Commissioner Carl Jacob Burckhardt expressly of his plans on 11th August 1939.
'Everything I undertake is directed against the Russians. If the West is too stupid and blind to grasp this, then I shall be compelled to come to an agreement with the Russians, beat the West and then after their defeat turn against the Soviet Union with all my forces. '

Despite the fact that Hitler was making no secret of his plan to seize Russia, Stalin had no real grasp of what Hitler thought, felt or was planning. He thought they could get along. They had so far. The two dictators had signed a ten year non-aggression pact in 1939. Since then, they had been Allies of a kind, secretly making plans together to divide up Eastern Europe. They had jointly invaded Poland in September 1939 and then carved up the country into eastern and western zones under the terms of the German-Soviet Frontier Treaty. They had even staged joint victory parades through

then, for which a grateful West would eventually thank him bountifully.

This mighty invasion would be, in Hitler's dreaming, a very different kind of war to that he had so far waged in the West. This would be Rassenkampf (Race War) and it would be a *'Total War'*. As the German Armed forces rolled east, they would simply exterminate the inferior races they encountered and — to use a more modern phrase — ethnically cleanse the land. All Jewish men and Communist party officials were to be killed on sight. Nothing elaborate would be necessary. Shooting would do. Any captured resistance fighters would likewise be executed without mercy and reprisals taken against the local community. Ordinary Slavs would be ruthlessly brutalised and deprived of food, resources and shelter until they succumbed to the inevitable. If they could flee east of the Ural mountains, Hitler just might —

the still smouldering rubble of Polish towns and cities. Stalin had not taken advantage and turned on Germany when its attention was fixed on the Western Blitzkrieg and Hitler had no complaints when the Soviet Union occupied and illegally annexed the three Baltic states of Lithuania, Latvia and Estonia a month later at the cost of over 160,000 civilian lives. Being basically a cheap gangster, Stalin thought that Hitler would be happy as long as he got his share of the booty. He simply could not grasp that Hitler was an ideologue who thought in very different terms.

In October 1940, the Russian tyrant was busy corresponding with the German Foreign Minister Ulrich Friedrich Wilhelm Joachim von Ribbentrop, enthusing about making existing Nazi/Soviet agreements permanent in everyone's best interests. He even made positive moves towards joining Germany as part of the Axis. In November 1940, Stalin went so far as to submit a formal paper laying out his plans for joining Hitler's side in the war. Great dictators together. Hitler never bothered to reply.

DISTRACTIONS, DISTRACTIONS...

Adolf Hitler was quite naturally delighted by the success of the German Blitzkrieg of May 1940 (for which he credited his own tactical genius), seizing France in just six weeks and knocking it out of the war. However, by the summer of 1940, as the Luftwaffe hammered away at the RAF over Southern England in preparation for invasion, his commanders found him decidedly lukewarm over the prospects of seizing Britain. He was uncharacteristically unenthusiastic about the whole thing and kept changing his mind.

The problem was that Hitler had never really considered Britain an enemy. The British were largely racially tolerable and had built a mighty empire that the Führer rather admired. If it wasn't for the recent appointment of Winston Churchill as prime minister, he might even have been able to reach some kind of compromise with them. How he resented them declaring war on him in 1939 just for invading Poland — and for not bowing to his will now.

Most of all, Hitler resented expending time and resources on subduing Britain. He wanted, in that summer of 1940, to be somewhere else entirely. He wanted to be waging war on Soviet Russia — the real enemy. All Hitler wanted was to get started on Lebensraum.

On 21st July, Hitler got particularly fidgety and impatient and asked General von Jodl, Chief of the Operations Staff of the High Command of the Armed Forces, if it would be possible to invade Russia in a couple of months time. Jodl explained that there wouldn't be enough time to plan and that

the summer of 1941 would be more feasible. Hitler grudgingly accepted his judgement but couldn't stop being obsessed. Just a week later, Hitler was in a meeting with his military commanders and telling them what he really, really wanted to do above all else was invade the Soviet Union.

Hitler formally issued a directive to invade Russia on 18th December 1940. While the plans were being drawn up, the operation was loosely referred to as 'Operation Otto' or 'Operation Fritz'. It was Hitler himself who renamed it Barbarossa — the nickname of Germanic emperor Frederick 1st. Hitler had a sense of deep history about him in these auspicious times.

OPPOSITE PAGE: German anti-communist propaganda poster, "Hands Off Europe"

ABOVE: Soviet propaganda poster, by S. Bochkov & S. Boym 'Let's Destroy The Fascist Invaders!', 1941

1941

ДАВАЙТЕ ПОБОЛЬШЕ ТАНКОВ,
ПРОТИВОТАНКОВЫХ РУЖЕЙ И ОРУДИЙ,
САМОЛЕТОВ, ПУШЕК, МИНОМЕТОВ,
СНАРЯДОВ, ПУЛЕМЕТОВ, ВИНТОВОК!

ВСЕ ДЛЯ ФРОНТА!
ВСЕ ДЛЯ ПОБЕДЫ!

IT WILL ALL BE OVER BY CHRISTMAS

Hitler was extremely confident that any attack launched against the Soviet Union would be a resounding success — and the whole enterprise would take just a matter of a few months. There were a number of factors that supported his assessment of the situation.

Firstly, the German Army had proved itself a hugely powerful force during the Blitzkrieg of May 1940 through the Low Countries and France and the tactics of Blitzkrieg themselves had proven extraordinarily successful and potent. The May Blitzkrieg was waged against the French and British. Warrior peoples. How much more effective would it be when unleashed against stupid and racially inferior races?

Secondly, Josef Stalin had wrecked his own Red Army in a series of ferocious and utterly paranoid purges beginning in 1937. He had fired, imprisoned or executed over 35,000 of his own officers, usually on the most flimsy of pretexts. They were *'enemies of the people'* — a catch all charge that could mean practically anything. Those who now held positions of command did so in a perpetual state of low morale and stark terror. Baffled by his behaviour, Hitler had suggested to Goebbels that *'Stalin is probably sick in the brain'*. Stalin's murder of a number of his own relatives only further convinced Hitler that Stalin was little short of a lunatic and could not adequately command a nation at war.

If further proof were needed of the Red Army's weakness, one only had to look at the recent war between the Soviets and the Finns. In November 1939, Russia had invaded the little nation of Finland, with the aim of absorbing them into the Soviet Union. Despite the Red Army enjoying numerical superiority of 3 to 1, they were devastated. The Finns fought a brilliant guerrilla war in their deep, dark, icy forests, combining ambush with sabotage. Soviet losses were horrendous. Stalin's strategic solution was to have many of his own commanders executed. It didn't help. By the time the Soviet Union consolidated what few gains it could make by flooding in troops (and now enjoying a 5 to 1 advantage), forcing the Finns to sign a messy peace treaty in March 1940, it had lost 220,000 soldiers. Finnish casualties were put at around 25,000. If the Russians could not even fight the Finns, how much worse might they fare against a professional war

ABOVE: "Everything for the Front. Everything for Victory". Soviet propaganda poster, 1941

To 9 July   To 1 September   To 9 September   To 5 December

ABOVE: Soviet soldiers emerge with raised hands from a burning armoured vehicle, during Operation Barbarossa

RIGHT: Winston Churchill giving the famous gesture

machine like the Wehrmacht?

So Barbarossa was certain to succeed. It wasn't even a gamble. Many of Hitler's commanders shared his optimism. General Jodl, for example boasted :

'The Russian colossus will be proved to be a pig's bladder. Prick it and it will burst'.

Everyone expected the Red Army to be devastated in just weeks far to the West of Moscow. The Soviet Union would then desperately sue for peace on whatever terms the Führer might generously grant them. There was one major concern however — the sheer distance that the Wehrmacht would need to cover. Moscow was, after all, almost 1,000 miles from Berlin. Supply lines would never cope and it was entirely possible that German industrial output could not keep pace with the demands of waging such a far-reaching campaign. Hitler reassured everyone that this was not really a problem. His armies would simply live off the land, taking food, fuel and other supplies from the people they conquered. He intended to starve them anyway and plunder seven million tons of grain every year from the breadbasket of Russia, the Ukraine (as well as abundant oil from the oilfields of the Caucasus). As the Germans plundered their supplies, the Soviets would have nothing to feed themselves with and they would die even sooner. One intelligence report, from May 1941, anticipated that 30 million Russians would starve to death. And that was just in the North of the country. Then Secretary to Rudolph Hess, Martin Bormann, agreed, saying, *'Many tens of millions will starve'.* Hitler thought this plan was yet more evidence of his genius — the need to plunder would actually kill his opponents even faster.

This seemed to satisfy the majority of the doubters and the Germans set about planning for the forthcoming invasion with enthusiasm and vigour. In fact, Hitler and his high command were so sure of swift and absolute success that they didn't even bother to order winter clothing for the troops.

INTELLIGENCE

Three million German troops (half the entire German Army) together with a further million soldiers from other Axis nations including Romania, Hungary, Slovakia and Finland, 3,350 Panzers and 7,000 field guns all moving into place is a very hard thing to conceal — as were 600,000

horses to pull the guns and much of the required supplies. Everybody could now see that Germany was preparing for an invasion of the east — everyone except Josef Stalin.

Stalin thought the German invasion preparations were just too obvious. He thought the Germans — if they were doing anything at all — were just winding him up. A lot of the German war industries needed minerals and resources from the east. Perhaps, Stalin reasoned, they were just trying to strong-arm him into keeping up the vital supply. Stalin was not even convinced that the Germans disliked him or his regime. He had followed a policy of appeasement to keep them happy — signing a non-aggression pact, sharing the spoils of Poland, letting them use Russian naval bases and supplying them with raw materials. Why spoil a good thing?

It didn't matter to him that — in the course of a month — he had received no less than eighty different warnings of an impending German invasion from everyone from the Dutch Communist Party to shadowy figures in the Balkans. Even British Intelligence warned him — but he had dismissed what they told him as a filthy trick perpetrated by that arch-imperialist Churchill. That capitalist lackey was just trying to provoke Stalin into declaring war on Germany and taking the pressure off Britain, which was being choked to death by Hitler's Atlantic U-Boat Wolf Packs and pounded each night by Göring's Luftwaffe. In Stalin's mind, Churchill's

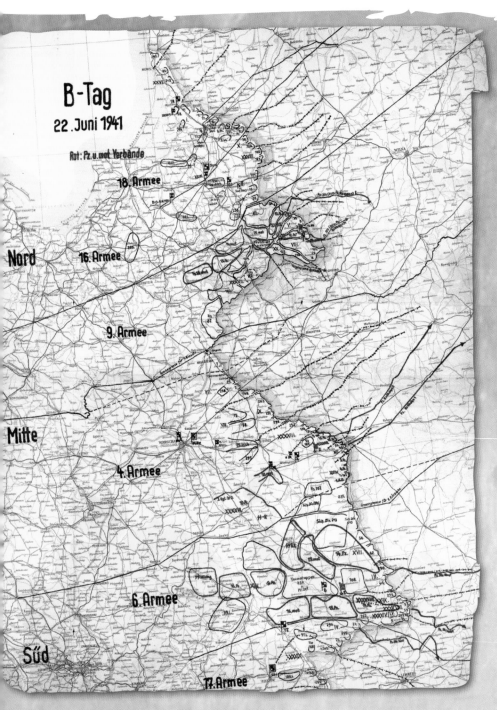

B-Tag
22.Juni 1941

Rot: Pz.u.mot.Verbände

Nord

18. Armee

16. Armee

9. Armee

Mitte

4. Armee

Süd

6. Armee

17. Armee

der Schulenburg — no friend to Hitler — had warned the Soviets. Stalin blithely dismissed his warnings as disinformation too.

Most of all, Stalin refused to listen to the many, many warnings because they contradicted his own strategic vision. It would, he had decided, be much more convenient for the Germans to invade (if they were coming) in late 1942 or early 1943 when his military preparations would finally be in place. So that's when the Germans would come.

DELAYS

Operation Barbarossa was all set to go in May 1941 but Hitler was forced to delay it because of a military coup in Yugoslavia which had deposed his ally. German troops despatched to restore *'order'* were then further diverted to Greece to repair Mussolini's grossly bungled attempts at invasion there. Hitler was furious with him. Hitler neither respected or trusted Il Duce, and indeed gave him just 30 minutes warning of Barbarossa when it began. For his part, a highly slighted Mussolini is on record as saying he hoped German casualties would be high. He could never imagine they might lose.

OPERATION BARBAROSSA

'We have only to kick in the door and the whole rotten structure will come crashing down'

Adolf Hitler

Barbarossa was finally launched in the early hours of Sunday 22nd June 1941 along a front stretching from the Baltic in the North to the Black Sea in the South heralded by massive artillery barrages and commando raids seizing or destroying important border targets. Each German soldier had been provided with a handy phrase book instructing how to say essential phrases in Russian including *'I'll shoot'*, *'Hands up!'* and *'Where is the collective farm chairman?'*. Despite this, most of the soldiers poised to attack believed the rumours that Barbarossa was just an elaborate diversion to conceal the invasion of Great Britain and they would probably not even be required to fire a shot in anger.

The Luftwaffe took off in waves targeting Soviet armoured formations, regional command centres and communication posts. Their chief targets

oafish tactics were just too obvious.

Reports from his own Russian spies stationed around the world started to cross Stalin's desk saying that the Germans intended to invade in May 1941. He ignored them. More urgent reports followed in June, most notably from a mole inside the Luftwaffe. Russia was to be attacked *'at any moment'*. Stalin dismissed this highly placed German source as a *'disinformant'*. A fortnight before the invasion, the German ambassador to Moscow, Count von

ABOVE + OPPOSITE PAGE:
Operation Barbarossa map

though were Soviet airfields — and they managed to catch and destroy over 1,000 Russian aircraft on the ground in just the first few hours of the attack. Soviet fighter pilots who did manage to take off were no match for the Luftwaffe fighters. The following day, the Luftwaffe accounted for another 1,000 Soviet warplanes.

The German forces surged east on a front 1800 km long. It was such a massive advance that — had anyone been up there — it would have been visible from space — and the attack was broadly divided into three:

Army Group North under Field Marshal von Leeb would attack the Baltic States and the Northern Soviet city of Leningrad. It was comprised of the 16th and 18th Armies and the 4th Panzer Group.

Army Group Centre (2nd and 3rd Panzer Groups, 2nd, 4th and 9th Armies) under Field Marshal von Bock would provide the thrust towards Moscow itself, striking at Minsk and Smolensk along the way.

Army Group South under Field Marshal von Rundstedt and comprising the 6th, 11th and 17th Armies supported by the 1st Panzer Group, would head south into the Ukraine, seizing the vast riches of crops, capturing Kiev and then heading down even further south to capture the oil fields of the Caucasus.

Behind them would follow the Einsatzgruppen. Part of the SS and formed by SS-Obergruppenführer Reinhard Heydrich (under the overall command of Heinrich Himmler), their specific task was to identify Jewish civilians and communist officials in the newly conquered territories — and kill them. Four different Einsatzgruppen were formed, each comprising around 900 men, to take part in Operation Barbarossa. In this task, they were aided by further battalions of the of the Order Police (Ordnungspolizei)

Everything went perfectly for the Germans. The Russians were utterly unprepared and even unwilling to fight. They had actually received direct instructions from Comrade Stalin just a few months ago not to rise to any provocation and aggression shown by the Germans and so in many cases were terrified to fight back lest they upset their great leader. They died in droves.

BARBAROSSA +1

The morning after, Stalin got news of the invasion and refused to believe it. So sure was he that Hitler would never go against him that he first assumed the reported invasion was the act of some rogue German generals. Five minutes later he changed his mind and decided that all the reports of a

massive German advance was just a cunning provocation to try to get him to be hostile to the Germans. Five minutes after that, he was on the phone to the foreign ministry trying to get the Japanese to talk to the Germans to tell them to stop. Stalin was deeply confused. He was, as Goebbels put it, like a rabbit mesmerised by a snake.

ALL ACCORDING TO PLAN

Initially everything went just as predicted. Although the Germans almost immediately slammed into Soviet armies of almost of the same numerical strength positioned close to the border, the German Blitzkrieg tactics — combined with a series of large encircling movements — proved devastating. Vast numbers of Soviets were efficiently surrounded in what the Germans termed Kessels ('Cauldrons') and destroyed.

The Soviets for their part quickly found their equipment and armaments markedly inferior to the Germans and their largely inexperienced commanders woefully incapable of dealing with intensive, fast-paced and wide ranging attacks. Because of Stalin's purges, around 75% had been in their posts for under a year and were clueless. Soviet soldiers surrendered everywhere. (In just the first seven months of the war, almost three million Russian soldiers would be captured). Casualties were horrendous. Those not killed or captured spilled back in an ungainly and chaotic retreat in their tens and hundreds of thousands. Field commanders commandeered transport and deserted their men. On day one alone, parts of the German army advanced a full 60 km into hostile territory.

Of the three German thrusts, Army Group Centre enjoyed the best results. Within less than a week, they had swept over 650 km east from the border, trapping more than 300,000 Soviet soldiers and destroying 2,500 pieces of enemy armour. By 11th July, 324,000 more Soviet soldiers were trapped in pockets around Minsk and Bialystok and German armour was sweeping across the Dnieper River. By 5th August, all Soviet defences around Smolensk had been effectively crushed and with them the Soviet 16th and 20th Armies. German panzers were now just 200 miles from the gates of Moscow.

In the North, panzers under von Manstein had progressed 50 miles in just the first day and swiftly crossed the Dvina River, near Dvinsk, and were half way to Leningrad in less than a week. Partisan groups from the Baltic States — conquered by Russia barely a year ago — rose up against the Red Army and joined in the fight.

Army Group South though achieved significantly less success. The Soviets were at their strongest here and managed to inflict heavy casualties on the invaders. Panzer forces also encountered the monstrous Soviet KV tanks for the first time as well as the new medium T-34s — and found them anything but a pushover. (War was particularly brutal here with neither side taking many prisoners and the Soviets additionally executing their own political prisoners before the Germans could free them.)

Just 12 days into the invasion, Chief of the German Army General Staff Franz Halder recorded in his diary,

'It is thus probably no understatement to say that the Russian Campaign has been won in the space of two weeks'.

ABOVE: German infantry advance during Operation Barbarosa, July 1941

ABOVE: German tank crew inspects a destroyed Soviet tank near Minsk

RIGHT: General Franz Halder

By July 14th, Hitler was so confident of success that he actually issued a directive suggesting that the army might be *'considerably reduced in the near future'*. In his mind, Russia was as good as done and he was already thinking of switching his resources to more ships and planes to deal with his last enemy — Britain — in the very near future. In this, he was slow to change his opinion. As late as September 1941, he still gave instructions to his High Command to consider the disbanding of as many as 40 divisions of the Wehrmacht.

Within three weeks across the three fronts, the Germans succeeded in destroying 3,500 pieces of Soviet armour, annihilating in excess of 6,000 Soviet fighters and bombers and killing or capturing two million Soviet soldiers. Following the tanks and the troops came the Einsatzgruppen, hunting down and executing Jews and communists wherever they found them. The ethnic cleansing began almost as the first shots were fired.

Around the world, everyone braced for a stunning (and inevitable) Nazi victory. In Britain, the War Office briefed the BBC not to give the public the impression that the Soviets could hold out for more than six more weeks. In America, Navy Intelligence told President Roosevelt that the Soviet Union could only hope to survive for another two months at best. In Whitehall, privately Churchill predicted that Moscow would be *'gone..'* by the end of the year at the very best. Everyone agreed, it was virtually all over.

THE THOUGHTS OF CHAIRMAN STALIN

Now, in strict secrecy, Stalin tried to see if he could buy the Germans off. He instructed the NKVD (his secret service) to find out — through the Bulgarian ambassador — why Germany had started the war and what price would they want to stop it. Would the territories of the Balkan States, the Ukraine, Bessarabia, Bukovina and the Karelian Peninsula be enough to make them happy — and if not — what else would they like? It was the most abject of surrender proposals and when it failed to gain any traction, Stalin would later try again in October 1941. (After the war, when news of these events broke, it was claimed that the Soviet leadership was just playing for time and didn't mean it really…).

On 27th June 1941, Stalin called a meeting of his top military commanders in Moscow, including General Georgy Zhukov, a peasant who was a truly formidable tactician and one of the few people who could answer back to Stalin and live. When it became clear that no-one had the first idea what was going on or where any of the competing armies actually were, Zhukov

lead the motherland to victory.

And it would be the motherland. Pretty early on, Stalin had come to the realisation that few of his people were willing to make the ultimate sacrifice for Communism or the Soviet State. They had to pretend to love it, largely to avoid imprisonment, torture or death, but few actually believed in it. Now he decided to promote the unfolding events as 'The Great Patriotic War' — nationalism was strong in the Russian heart. People who would not stand and fight for the Soviet Union would gladly die for Mother Russia. Comrades now became Brothers and Sisters in more and more of Stalin's speeches. In response, four million Russians volunteered for the Opolchentsy militia. Stalin said thank you and rapidly sent them off in many cases without even uniforms or weapons to face German armour. They were slaughtered.

THE WORST OF FRIENDS

In Britain, Winston Churchill was frankly relieved to see Russia being forced to enter the war. Soviet Russia was not the ally he sought — that was America — but it would do. He thought Stalin an oaf and tyrant but, for the sake of expediency he would now *'befriend'* him. *'If Hitler invaded Hell, I would at least make a favourable reference to the Devil in the House of Commons,'* Churchill said, leaving little doubts as to who Satan might be in this metaphor. Josef Stalin became *'Uncle Joe'*, the avuncular ally whom you could imagine sitting around the radio with — instead of a cold blooded mass murder who had already butchered in the Ukraine far more people than Hitler's Holocaust would ever consume.

Despite his doubts that Stalin could long hold out against the might of Germany, Churchill started promising — and delivering — war supplies to the Soviets, for which in truth Stalin was both boldly ungrateful and haughtily unimpressed. What he wanted was a second front, for Britain to invade Occupied France and by drawing German forces west to fight Britain to take the pressure off the Red Army. He would keep calling for it, monotonously and aggressively, until D-Day in 1944.

BUTCHERY

Heinrich Heydrich had told the Einsatzgruppen that all Jews wherever they were to be found were to be regarded as resistance fighters and ordered the killing of all Jewish males between 15 and 45 years of age. (Additionally all Red Army prisoners from Georgia and Central Asia were also to be murdered,

burst into tears and Stalin stormed out, returning home to his private dacha. He stayed there for two days, refusing to see anyone, until a contingent of his most loyal followers enticed him out with the promise that only he could

on the off-chance they were Jewish.) This ruling lasted for only a couple of weeks before Jewish women and children were also being shot.

At the same time, the Einsatzgruppen were given instructions to try and incite racial hatred against Jews in the native populations of conquered territories and to start murderous pogroms. In this they were successful. The Einsatzgruppen managed to ignite some 40 different pogroms in just the first few weeks of Barbarossa, resulting in the death of 10,000 Jews.

By August, mass execution by firing squad was proving too slow, so machine guns and sub-machine guns were substituted for rifles and large groups of victims sprayed with bullets before any survivors were finished off with a pistol shot to the head. By September, the Einsatzgruppen found themselves seriously frustrated by the fact that they could not keep up with the sheer numbers of Jews who needed killing. Instead, they suggested that Jewish captives to be used for slave labour tasks until such times as they could be disposed of properly.

WARNING SIGNS

The problems that the Germans would face later in the campaign started to become evident in the first couple of months of the war, even as the Germans were still achieving stunning victories.

The sheer scale of the operation had never been properly appreciated and the Wehrmacht was getting strung out and stretched. Slower units could not keep up with the faster, more mobile ones. Panzer units quickly found themselves far ahead of their supporting infantry and had to stop and sit around until the infantry could catch up

'*The vastness of Russia devours us,*' said Field Marshal von Rundstedt,   beginning to feel uneasy and far, far, far from home.

Supplying the far-flung units was proving difficult, even in fine weather. The Russian roads were poor and could not cope with constant lorry convoys. The idea of the army '*living*

OPPOSITE PAGE: Propaganda poster by Kukryniksy 'Destroy the enemy mercilessly'

ABOVE: An Einsatzgruppe D soldier about to shoot a Jewish man kneeling at a partially filled mass grave in Vinnitsa, Ukraine SSR

off the land' was also proving to be impossible. There was nowhere near enough fuel to be found locally for motorised and armoured units and the peasant population were often hungry themselves. They could be robbed of all their possessions — perhaps a pig or some eggs and chickens (and condemned to starve to death) — but what use was that to an entire army? What's more, as the Red Army had fallen back it had — wherever possible — employed 'Scorched Earth' tactics — destroying wells and supplies of crops, slaughtering livestock and trying to render useless anything else that the Germans might need or want. Dedicated 'Destruction Battalions' were assigned to the task, while units of the NKVD hunted down and murdered those who they thought might be future collaborators or political prisoners who might be of use to the Germans.

The sheer distances that needed to be traversed also proved to be at odds with German Blitzkrieg tactics. By the end of August, the German Army had sustained around 400,000 losses and the panzer divisions had suffered more combat casualties than ever anticipated. Now it proved that — while Blitzkrieg was useful for a short, sharp war, it could not be kept up indefinitely. The attrition it produced was just too great. There simply were not enough men and materials to sustain three German combat forces fighting their way East. Hard choices would have to be made. And sacrifices.

General Halder, so optimistic in the first fortnight of the war was rapidly having second thoughts. In August, he complained *'The Russian Colossus ...has been underestimated by us'.* And there were more enemies than anyone had ever suspected. German intelligence had estimated Soviet strength in the path of the invasion forces to be about 200 divisions. By mid-August, the Wehrmacht had already encountered 360 enemy divisions and knew that there must be many more out there.

Before Barbarossa, German tank commanders had not even heard of a Soviet medium tank called the T-34. Now they were astonished by its prowess on the battlefield. It could move fast, manoeuvre well and — despite its status as a medium tank, carry enough armour so that tank shells would simply bounce off it. Compared to the British and French armour encountered during 1940, this was something altogether different. For the first time, an opponent had tanks as good as the Panzer Groups.

THE FIRST ARCTIC CONVOY

The first convoy from Britain carrying aid to the Soviets set out from Scarpa Flow on 21st August, sailing through arctic waters to arrive in Russia on August 31st. The seven ship convoy carried a number of Hawker Hurricane fighters as well as a mixture of other supplies.

TACTICAL CONFUSION

In August 1941, Hitler met with his senior generals in East Prussia to decide how to conduct the next phase of the campaign. Unfortunately for the Führer (and indeed his generals), Hitler had a chronic dose of diarrhoea and was not in the best frame of mind. It seemed like, every time he returned from the toilet he would have a new priority for his men to deliver. One time it would be the capture of Moscow. The next Leningrad would be the priority. Then he would dash off and return a few minutes later with emphatic demands to protect the flank of Army Group Centre at all costs or perhaps to destroy the Soviet industrial base before all else.

In private, Hitler was starting to worry about the quality of German intelligence and he was already comprehending that Russia might have far more resources to call upon than German Intelligence had ever detected.

Despite his High Command advising he head for Moscow, it concerned him that the Soviets had now put 900,000 men between his armies and the capital. It was, in the whole campaign, where they were now strongest. Might it not be a good idea then to strike where the Soviets were weaker?

Towards the end of August, Hitler finally firmed up his priorities. Leningrad would be the priority rather than Moscow, with Reinhardt's Panzers sent north and extra resources devoted to destroying the Soviet forces in the south. To this end, Army Group Centre would lend the Panzers of Heinz Guderian's Panzer Group 2 to Army Group South, instead of using them to drive on to Moscow. The period became known to military historians as 'Hitler's Summer Pause'. Halder would call it, *'the greatest strategic blunder of the Eastern campaign'*. Following the decision, Franz Halder then had a complete nervous collapse, but had the common sense to do it out of sight of the Führer.

SAVING SOVIET INDUSTRY

In a move that German Intelligence had never anticipated, the Soviets took to disassembling their production facilities in the path of German forces and sending critical manufacturing plant eastwards by rail to be reassembled and reused in new facilities in the Ural Mountains and Siberia, far out of reach of the guns and the bombers.

ABOVE: Headquarters of the Commander of the Army Field Marshal von Brauchitsch. L-R Field Marshal Keitel, Field Marshal von Brauchitsch ,Hitler, Gen. Colonel Halder

OPPOSITE PAGE: Field Marshal Gerd von Rundstedt

KIEV

Guderian's Panzer Group headed south into the Ukraine as instructed and won an overwhelming victory in Kiev — the third largest city in the Soviet Union. Over 400,000 Soviets were taken prisoner as the city fell on 18th September, trapped by brilliantly-executed German encirclement tactics which saw them advance for another 150 miles beyond the city. Despite the earnest advice from Zhukov to let the troops escape, Stalin had ordered them to stand and fight to the last man. He changed his mind at the last minute but it was far too late. It was a total disaster and a stunning victory for the Germans.

Hitler took it as evidence of his own tactical genius and proclaimed it *'the greatest battle in the history of the world'*. Many of his generals thought it was an irrelevancy. Hitler should have gone for Moscow instead.

Less than 2 weeks later, 33,771 Jewish civilians from Kiev were massacred in the ravine of Babi Yar beyond the city limits. They had come forward when called to do so, unaware of the Nazi's genocidal tendencies. Although the murders were carried out by the Einsatzgruppen and elements of the Waffen-SS, it was with the active connivance of the regular Wehrmacht.

HAIL THE CONQUERORS

In many territories conquered by the Germans in 1941 — but perhaps especially in the Ukraine — there was initial enthusiasm for their arrival. Many of the diverse peoples they encountered hated Communism, hated the Soviet Union and hated Stalin. The Germans, they hoped, might be their liberators. Their hopes were soon dashed. To their new German occupiers, they were racially inferior — an unforgivable sin. The Germans abused them mercilessly. They performed mass executions. They initiated programmes of starvation. They tyrannised and they terrified — and in that way they lost the potential

ABOVE LEFT: Men of the Advance Guard sweep an occupied Soviet village for Soviet soldiers and snipers

ABOVE MIDDLE: Victims of war, Grushki district. Ukraine, Kiev

ABOVE RIGHT: Erich Koch

BELOW: Russian unit captured in battle is marched to a shed for interrogation. Kiev,

BOTTOM RIGHT: Ukrainian poster depicting a German soldier protecting a Ukrainian woman, targeted at colonists of the Reichsgau Wartheland

good will and support which they could have used to their significant advantage had they only thought to be a little more kind and a little less genocidal. When, in September 1941, Erich Koch (an ardent Nazi and leading Christian who had achieved the rank of Praeses of Synod of the old-Prussian Ecclesiastical Province of East Prussia) was appointed to the Ukrainian Commissariat, he proudly announced:

'I am known as a brutal dog ... Our job is to suck from Ukraine all the goods we can get hold of ... I am expecting from you the utmost severity towards the native population.'

Among his many achievements in administering the Ukraine were to shut all the schools, saying *'Ukraine children need no schools. What they'll have to learn will be taught them by their German masters..'*

who were:

'A master race, which must remember that the lowliest German worker is racially and biologically a thousand times more valuable than the population here.'

The self-proclaimed 'brutal dog' was later sentenced to be put down by a Polish court in 1959, due to his association with the murder of 400,000 Poles in the death camps but the order was never carried out *'on the grounds of ill health'*. He died in captivity in 1986.

НІМЕЦЬКИЙ ВОЇН БОРЕТЬСЯ ЗА ЕВРОПУ

МИ ПОМАГАЕМО ПЕРЕМОГТИ ЗАБЕЗПЕЧЕННЯМ ЖНИВ

FIGHTING THE PARTISANS

Josef Stalin had called for bands of loyal civilian comrades to take up arms against the Germans within a fortnight of Operation Barbarossa starting. The Partisan movement did not enjoy an auspicious start, because there were few capable resistance fighters around, thanks to internal repression within the Soviet Union. That is, Stalin had had most of them shot already. The early partisan movements further suffered from a chronic lack of good weaponry. Despite this, and despite the prior Soviet executions of those with aggression and initiative, by the end of 1941 there was believed to be some 72,000 partisans active in the field. Most operated totally independently of Moscow and had no means of communicating with — and thereof co-operating with — the army. Nevertheless, the Partisans grew to become a potent enough force for Nazi Germany to launch a number of large scale operations against them in early 1942, such as Operation Hanover.

As Stalin grew more enthusiastic about the Partisans, they were offered support where possible but much of the time would have to rely on seizing supplies either from the Germans they killed — or their own people. To many inside the ravaged Soviet Union, the partisans were every bit as murderous as the Germans. They would terrorise the local civilians, set up their own kangaroo courts and steal, rape and pillage all in the name of the 'Motherland'. Comrades could be executed just for having no faith in the inevitable victory of Mother Russia. Women who had been raped by the Germans were now condemned as 'collaborators' by the Partisans — before being raped again and then shot. In the judgement of many, the Partisans were worse than the Nazis. The Nazis would kill in cold blood — but with Partisans it was personal. They might want to take their time, and to torture first.

To add to the confusion — and the motivation to murder — there were partisan groups who hated both the Nazis and the Communists. The Ukraine, for example had its own nationalist partisan units who would wage war both on the Germans and the regular Russian partisans.

When partisans were successful in raids and ambushes on German forces, the Germans would often order direct reprisals against the nearest village. While the people were executed, the partisans would be safely away in the thick of the forest and nothing was achieved. There were calls from high ranking German generals to end support for the partisans by treating the local population better, but Hitler was having none of that, saying:

'Only where the struggle against the partisan nuisance was begun and carried out with ruthless brutality have successes been achieved'.

RIGHT: Three young partisan women, collective farmers discuss tactics

ABOVE: Wearied motorcyclists using the time for a short rest. September 1941

He wanted them to be nothing less than totally annihilated. It was never achieved. By 1944, there were thought to be half a million partisans fighting the Germans behind their lines.

THE SIEGE OF LENINGRAD

After an earlier attack on Leningrad had been successfully resisted and held 100 km from the city in mid-July, the siege of the northern city of Leningrad (formerly known as St Petersburg) began on 8th September 1941 when it was effectively surrounded by elements of Army Group North operating in conjunction with Finnish forces located to the North. It had already been subjected to intense shelling since 20th August and attempts by civilians to flee the city by rail and road had been halted by aggressive long ranging German units. The siege would not be lifted until 27th January 1944 and during those 872 days more than one million civilians would perish, 400,000 of them children.

Army Group North were given very clear instructions by Adolf Hitler about how to treat Leningrad. He had no interest in seeing the city survive and having to feed its worthless inhabitants. If the city offered to surrender, such surrender should not be accepted. German intelligence had calculated that the city would crumble due to mass starvation within just a few weeks. The Axis forces would simply sit outside the city perimeters and wait, launching both air raids and artillery bombardments into the city to increase the suffering of the largely civilian populace and hasten the collapse of morale. Inside, the crisis situation was exacerbated by the recent arrival by as many as 300,000 desperate and homeless refugees from outlying towns which had now fallen under Nazi control.

On 12th September, disaster struck when German artillery destroyed the largest food depot in the city.

CRIMEA ISOLATED

By 25th September, German forces in the Ukraine had managed to drive a wedge between the nation and the Crimean Peninsula. 32,000 independent Soviet Maritime Army soldiers under the command of Major-General Pretov would spend the next two months building massive fortifications around the strategic city of Sevastopol, in anticipation of the expected German drive down into the peninsula. The attack came as expected, with von Manstein electing to occupy much of the peninsula while manoeuvring cautiously around Sevastopol itself and not attempting an all-out assault on the well-protected city.

EINSATZGRUPPEN AND ARMY GROUP NORTH

In the Baltic States, Einsatzgruppen A set about executing civilians with great enthusiasm. By the start of winter 1941, they proudly reported to Himmler that they had successfully killed precisely 136,421 Jews as well as 1,064 '*communists*'. For good measure, they had also shot 653 people with a mental illness. They were also successful in inciting a major pogrom against the Jews in Lithuania, partly by deliberately releasing violent criminals from the country's prisons. Foremost amongst them was a man who earned the nickname '*The Death Dealer of Kaunas*', who's speciality was to beat a bound and helpless Jewish captive to death with a crowbar, pausing between executions to play the assembled crowds a rendition of the Lithuanian national anthem on his accordion. In another inventive act of murder, the Rabbi of Slobodka was tied up, pressed face down into a copy of the Talmud and had his head sawn off while his wife and child watched. They were killed afterwards. In all, 4,000 Jews were murdered in just five days.

Latvia fared no better. It's estimated that out of 83,000 Jews rounded up by the Germans, perhaps no more than 900 survived. 25,000 Jews from Riga were massacred in just two days, as Himmler wanted Latvian Jews cleared out of the way so that the country could then receive shipments of German Jews to be '*dealt with*' conveniently out of sight.

The Commander of Einsatzgruppe A , Franz Stahlecker, was killed by Soviet partisans in 1942.

OPERATION TYPHOON

With the South of Russia now subjugated to a satisfactory degree, Hitler finally agreed to push on to Moscow. Operation Typhoon was planned — essentially a pincer attack on the capital city by forces from north and south involving almost 2 million soldiers, 1700 tanks and 600 aircraft of the Luftwaffe. However, Typhoon was fatally delayed by almost a month because of vital panzer forces having being diverted off to Leningrad and

OPPOSITE PAGE: Russian trenches on the Leningrad Front before an offensive

ABOVE LEFT: Major General Erich von Manstein

ABOVE RIGHT: Franz Walter Stahlecke

RIGHT: Soviet propaganda poster, 1941. The caption reads 'Let's Shield Leningrad with our Breasts!' Poster by A. Kokorekin

ГРУДЬЮ НА ЗАЩИТУ ЛЕНИНГРАДА!

the Ukraine on Hitler's earlier instructions and then needing to be recalled. More armour had been withdrawn from the battlefield for repair and maintenance and was coming back to the units more slowly than expected, due to the sheer distances involved, if nothing else.

The revised date for Typhoon was set at 30th September, with the aim of completely surrounding Moscow by 7th November. By the start of October 1941, the 3rd and 4th Panzer Groups had encircled no less than five Soviet armies around the town of Vyazma in what became known as the Vyazma pocket. As the trapped armies fought to break through the German ring, they were slaughtered. A further German victory close by at Bryansk effectively cleared the way to Moscow itself. In the two battles, the Germans took 660,000 prisoners and destroyed 1200 Soviet tanks.

The news of the twin victories were greeted with deep joy in Germany. Hitler thought the Red Army was now broken, while his Press Chief, Otto Dietrich, declared , *'for all military purposes Soviet Russia is done with.'*

On 3rd October 1941, Hitler made a speech of some significance after returning to Belin. He told the German people;

'I declare today, and I declare it without any reservation that the enemy in the East has been struck down and will never rise again.'

LEFT: German soldiers outside of Moscow during the 1941 Battle of Moscow

ABOVE: L-R Siegfried Uiberreither, Martin Bormann, Adolf Hitler & Otto Dietrich

MOSCOW IN PANIC

The capital was rapidly slipping into terror and chaos. Political prisoners were hastily shot, while a labour force of 250,000 — mostly women — were sent out to start digging anti-tank ditches.

On 16th October, Stalin and his most trusted cronies tried to leave Moscow in secret. They were spotted and now panic really set in. There were rumours of German troops already inside the city and some Muscovites even resorted to sticking willkommen signs in their windows. Thousands of their fellows simply swamped the trains at every railway station, quite literally fighting to get out. On 19th October, Stalin abandoned his plans to leave the city — and lashed out against the traitorous citizens who were trying to leave. Moscow was placed under a curfew and the NKVD given free rein to keep order in the city and deal with *'defeatists and cowards'* and *'panic-mongers'* by whatever means necessary. They interpreted it as the power to shoot any civilians on the spot for any reason they deemed necessary.

DOGS OF WAR

At the same time, a desperate new measure was unleashed against the Panzers. German tank crews were shocked to see dogs rushing eagerly towards their tanks and scuttle underneath. Seconds later, they would explode. The poor beasts had been trained to associate tanks with food and then had bombs strapped to their bodies. The Germans had to shoot them with their tank-mounted machine guns before they could come close. There

is some measure of justice however in the fact that, on more than a few occasions, the hapless dogs actively chose to run towards Soviet armour and blow it up instead. The Soviet tanks, it seemed, smelled familiar while the German armour, with its different blends of fuel and lubricants smelled *'foreign'.*

THE RAIN BEGINS

> *"If they want a war of extermination, they will have one.'*

Josef Stalin, 6th November

The most advanced German units were now closing in on Moscow. It seemed like nothing could stop them. Commanding Army Group Central, von Bock received explicit instructions on 10th October sealing the fate of the city:

> *'The Führer has reaffirmed his decision that the surrender of Moscow will not be accepted, even if it is offered by the enemy.'*

In other words, Moscow was to be destroyed rather than conquered. Strategic gaps would be left to let some of the people inside flee the destruction — but only to fill the roads and hamper the manoeuvrability of Soviet forces. The refugees were only good as anti-tank obstacles.

And then the driving late Autumn rains — the Rasputitza — began. For three weeks in mid-October and early November, the roads became almost

impassable and everything ground to a halt. Even the most mobile of units could only advance a maximum of 2 miles a day. The Germans tried everything — even using the stiff corpses of Russian dead as planks under their wheels — but nothing worked. Trucks and half-tracks bogged down, and horses stumbled, slipped and struggled in the deep liquid filth. The Germans cursed their foul luck while General Zhukov used the opportunity to steady his troops on the frontline.

'We have seriously underestimated the Russians, the extent of their country and the treachery of their climate. This is the revenge of reality' Guderian wrote home to his wife on 9th November.

THE ICE ROAD

In the besieged city of Leningrad, things were becoming increasingly desperate by November of 1941. When Lake Lagoda froze, the Soviets were finally able to establish an ice road — which they called the *'Road of Life'* over the lake but it was a tiny corridor at best and nowhere near capable of supplying a massive city. Leningrad was in the grip of starvation and rations had been restricted to just 125 grams of bread a day — and that was adulterated with 50% sawdust and other fillers. However, during the month of January 1942, while the lake remained solidly frozen, some 800,000 refugees would be evacuated to safety.

OPERATION TYPHOON RESUMES

The German commanders were actually relieved when the winter rains started to turn to snow, having no real idea what it foreshadowed. They resumed their advance on Moscow on 15th November, with the sodden roads now frozen solid and therefore slightly more negotiable. By 27th November, advanced German units were just 30 km from the city. By 1st December, one German battalion had reached the town of Kimkhi, only 8km away from the outskirts of the city. Moscow — and the spires of the Kremlin — was now literally within sight. By 5th December, everything had changed. Temperatures plummeted to less than — 20 degrees, accompanied by ferocious snowstorms and the Germans found it impossible to advance any further.

ABOVE: Colonel General Fedor von Bock

OPPOSITE PAGE:
BOTTOM LEFT + MIDDLE: A hastily assembled work force of Moscow women and elderly men gouge a huge tank trap out of the earth to halt German Panzers advancing on the Russian capital.

BOTTOM RIGHT: Soviet military dog training school in Moscow Oblast

THE FIRST RETREAT - ARMY GROUP SOUTH

In late November the 1st Panzer Group down in the Eastern Ukraine, battling in ferocious snowstorms, managed to seize the city of Rostov — the so called *'gateway'* to the Caucasus — but did not have the strength to hold it. Just five days later, they were forced to make a swift retreat by determined and clever Soviet opposition around the River Don at Rostov and did not stop until they reached the River Mius. It was the first time Germany had made any significant retreat since the start of the entire war in 1939. Hitler was, predictably furious. Field Marshal von Rundstedt offered his resignation and it was accepted immediately by the Führer. (Von Runstedt recalls in his diary simply, *'I then went home'*). Field Marshal Reichenau was appointed in his place — but within hours he too was recommending retreat. Hitler flew down to the Ukraine a few days later to find out for himself what was really going on.

THE WAR CHANGES

In November, Stalin had taken a huge gamble and started withdrawing some troops from the Far East to be shipped across the entire country and used instead to defend Moscow. They might well have been needed to fight against belligerent Japanese forces in an Asian war that everyone knew was coming — but Stalin wagered that the Japanese would be more interested in the Americans and European Colonial interests rather than his territories. He gambled right.

On 7th December 1941, the Japanese launched a surprise attack on the American Fleet and air bases at Pearl Harbor. This could have been disastrous news for the Soviets, but their spies soon determined that Japan did indeed intend to wage war to the south in the Pacific, concentrating on American and European forces and territories. They were simply not interested in fighting the Russians in the frigid wilderness to the north. At once, Stalin could release even more invaluable reserves of troops and materials from the Far East and have them shipped back to Moscow by rail, to take part in the defence of the city. Three days after Pearl Harbor, Hitler declared war on America — and Stalin suddenly had another ally in the war, one a lot more wealthy (and hopefully generous) in shipping off the war aid than contemptible Great Britain.

RIGHT: Field Marshal Walter von Reichenau discusses with Lieutenant General Stapf a situation report

ABOVE: Winter battle for Moscow, Soviet infantrymen advance

COUNTER ATTACK

The Soviet counter-attack against the German forces of Army Group Centre threatening Moscow started on 6th December. Nineteen Russian armies smashed in to von Bock's troops along a five hundred mile front. The attack was heralded by the chilling wail of Katyusha rockets and spearheaded by waves of dependable T-34 medium tanks which coped far better on frozen ground than any German armour. They were supported by Soviet aircraft, newly arrived and stored and maintained in Russian airfields with proper hangars. The assault coincided with a devastating drop in temperature. The Third Reich was about to find itself in combat not just with the Red Army but also with Russia's most ruthless commander — 'General Winter'. Most of the German forces had never experienced anything like ambient temperatures of -30 degrees Celsius, accompanied by lashing, blinding snowstorms and drifts deeper than a horse. The Soviet soldiers had. Within two days, the Red Army had advanced as much as 12 miles and forced 17 German motorised divisions into retreat.

Caught out in near Arctic conditions, the Germans immediately suffered from having no adequate winter clothing. Many were still in their light summer uniforms. Caught out in the open, some German units simply dug holes to offer the barest kind of protection and jumped in. The lucky ones lost toes and fingers to frost bite. The unlucky ones died in their sleep. Those with frostbite might find themselves disciplined as — by getting frostbite — they had proved themselves somehow disloyal to the Reich. The dead were beyond all discipline. Other units used their initiative. Where peasant hovels could be found, the owners would be robbed of every last rag to stuff down the German's battle tunics or wrap around their feet. Others would be ejected from their homes into the cold or else have their meagre dwellings broken down for firewood. Either way, they would die. Soviet POWs too were stripped of all their useful clothing and sent on their way to freeze to death.

The Germans suddenly found it almost impossible to fight. Their machine guns and rifles jammed. Gunsights froze solid. On the fields hastily converted into forward Luftwaffe bases, aircraft with no protection simply froze up solid and could not fly. Panzers began to seize up and lorries to break down. To get a tank engine to start, fires had to be lit underneath the vehicle to warm up the gasoline — not the safest of practices. Struggling horses died in harness, snowblind, their hearts giving out under the strain of hunger, blizzard temperatures and the effort of trying to haul artillery on slippery roads where they could gain no traction. When the artillery could be deployed, the guns simply froze up. Communications broke down as radios refused to work in the cruel temperatures. The Germans could call on virtually no reserves, but now the Soviet forces rushed from the Far East were joining the assault. To men used to fighting in Siberia, the temperatures around Moscow seemed positively balmy by comparison and, of course, they were supremely well equipped for winter warfare. Partisan units behind German lines joined in the attack, as did Soviet ski troops and even Cossack cavalry divisions. And they fought well, not at all like the Soviet units the Germans had encountered at the start of Barbarossa.

In response, some German units hastily retreated as much as 100 miles in less than a fortnight. In some places panic set in and German units were routed or fled. They left their frozen dead behind where they had perished. There was now no hope of taking Moscow in 1941. The best that could be achieved was a stabilising of German lines.

By mid-December, the German High Command realised just what trouble they were in and there were increasing threats of mutiny being reported. Hitler would not hear of any further retreat. With Christmas less than two weeks away, he ordered all German troops to stand their ground and told the commanders of Army Group Centre that their men need to develop a 'fanatical will'. By 16th December, the commander of Army Group Centre, Field Marshal von Bock, was actively requesting reassignment from his command. Other generals were simply fired by the Führer, particularly those whose commands had retreated without Hitler's permission. Panzer commander Guderian, the recent hero of Kiev, questioned the Führer's orders to try and save German lives and was quickly stripped of his command. The Commander in Chief of the Germany Army, Field Marshal von Brauchitsch, also a critic, suddenly resigned and was treated with nothing but contempt. Hitler behind his back referred to him as a vain cowardly wretch and a nincompoop and would later appoint himself Commander in Chief in his place. There was no one else who could do the job, he explained to Halder, because none of his generals were sufficiently National Socialist in their thoughts. Hitler later explained

'I had to act ruthlessly. I had to send even my closest generals packing, two army generals, for example ... I could only tell these gentlemen, 'Get yourself back to Germany as rapidly as you can but leave the army in my charge. And the army is staying at the front.'

The fight for Moscow in those brief few weeks from November 1941 to the start of January 1942 cost the Wehrmacht over a quarter of a million dead and a further half million wounded. Soviet losses during the fighting are believed to be approximately double. As General Halder later wrote;

'The myth of the invincibility of the German Army was broken'

HELFT
GEBT

SPINNSTOFF-WÄSCHE-UND KLEIDER=
SAMMLUNG 1944

BACK HOME

Grim news of the plight of the soldiers at the front soon spread back home to Germany, despite explicit orders to soldiers on leave to stay silent, Propaganda Minister Goebbels tried to make light of the situation by launching an appeal for German hausfraus to donate their fur coats. The coats did actually reach some soldiers towards the end of the year and were greeted with utter bafflement. Here were expensive high fashion items more suited to the salon and the opera being paraded by battered, exhausted men in rags and infested with lice.

NO RETREAT, NO SURRENDER

Since Stalin had decided to hold Moscow after all, the Red Army was similarly given instructions to stand and fight at all costs. If they fled the battlefield, they would run into rear-guard units with instructions to kill them. Field officers were also given orders to instantly execute any of their men showing cowardice. From somewhere warm, Stalin sat back, puffed on his pipe and smirked *'In the Soviet army, it takes more courage to retreat than to advance.'*

WAR IN THE SOUTH

On 17th December, von Manstein finally launched the long-anticipated assault on the fortress city of Sevastopol in the Crimea. Within a week he had managed to break through two of the formidable defensive rings surrounding the city. Just one remained. However, when significant Soviet reinforcements started moving in on him from the east, he decided not to press home his attack any further and called a halt on 28th December.

LITTLE HORRORS

On 29th December, Soviet forces overran a German field hospital at Feodosia. They then set about slaughtering the 160 German wounded to be found there. Some were thrown from high windows. Others were dragged outside, drenched in water and left to freeze.

TOP LEFT: Joseph Goebbels

TOP RIGHT: Propaganda poster encouraging the German public to donate clothing in order to support the Reich's war effort

BOTTOM LEFT: The Soviet cruiser Molotov at Sevastopol

BOTTOM MIDDLE: Members of Die Gebirgsjägertruppe, The Mountain Unit in Crimea

BOTTOM RIGHT: German soldiers interrogate civilians in Crimea

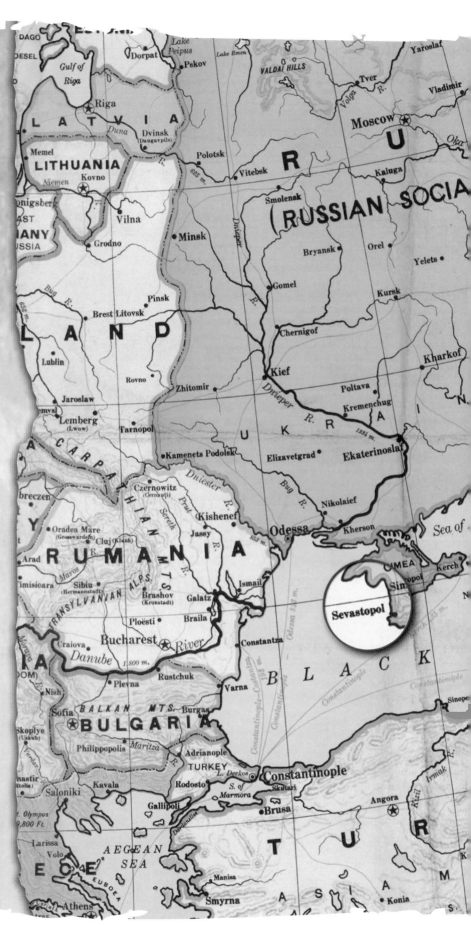

1942

FIGHTING BACK

On 5th January 5 1942, Stalin ordered an ambitious — and supremely impractical — further counter attack. The Red Army would, he said, counter-attack everywhere in what he called *'local offensives'* By the end of 1941, Stalin was convinced that the Germans had fatally over extended themselves and could be comprehensively defeated and destroyed by mid-1942. Despite Zhukov's protests, Stalin's instructions were obeyed and, predictably, the grand counter-attack very quickly ground to a halt. While weakened German forces were driven still further back from Moscow and the Soviets got close at some point to recapturing both Smolensk and Bryansk, little else was achieved.

The Soviets attacked again at the end of January, driving a hard wedge between elements of Army Groups North and Centre as they fought to retake Smolensk. Only a well-disciplined and well-organised action by the Germans managed to block their progress. To the north, the Soviet 2nd Shock Army attacked German positions on the Volkhov River. They were smashed by a ferocious German counterattack and their leader, Lieutenant General Andrey Vlasov, defected to the German side. However, Kursk was successfully retaken on 8th February, just days after German forces were driven once more from Rostov.

THE TRIUMPH OF THE WILL

Despite the Soviet counter-offensives, by the end of January 1942, the German armies spread out before Moscow were regaining some of their former confidence. They had survived the weather. They had survived whatever Stalin could throw at them and they were still there. Hitler ascribed

RIGHT: Soviet propaganda poster depicting a Russian soldier crawling through barbed wire with a hand grenade, the caption reads 'The German Tank Will Not Get Over Here!'. Poster by N. Zhukov

НЕМЕЦКИЙ ТАНК ЗДЕСЬ НЕ ПРОЙДЕТ

EASTERN FRONT 6-12-41 - 6-5-42

Soviet Gains   German Gains

this to his personal willpower, which he had manifested through the troops inspired by him.

Having thrown so much into the winter assault on Moscow, Hitler now decided that 1942 would concentrate on war in the south, with the objective of seizing the oilfields in the Caucasus. Once this territory was conquered, German forces could move even further south and seize Oil production centres in the Middle East as well as threaten the Suez Canal from the east as well as from the west. Army Group South would now be split into two — Army Groups A and B to concentrate on separate objectives.

THE EXTERMINATIONS CONTINUE

From the very start of the year, the Einsatzgruppen were engaged in yet another wave of extermination. Einsatzgruppe A, which had been so successful in wiping out the Jewish population of the Baltic States was now loaned to Einsatzgruppe B, attached to Army Group Central. They were deployed to Belarus, where, over the course of just four days, they reduced the Jewish population of the city of Dnepropetrovsk from 30,000 to 702, employing the help of local collaborators and German policemen to accomplish the task. This second wave of extermination met with at least some resistance from the Jews, but they had next to no weapons and all too often their former friends and neighbours would betray them. Some managed to escape though, and the deep woods provided a safe haven of a sort from which they could organise and even fight back.

THE FINAL SOLUTION

Ex-chicken farmer and now Reichsführer-SS Heinrich Himmler had realised within just weeks of Operation Barbarossa that the Einsatzgruppen were just not up to the task of exterminating European Jewry. Even though they had been recruited from 'hardcore' organisations including the SS and the Gestapo, significant numbers of them were becoming alarmingly unhinged by the task of shooting terrified men, women and children day in and day out. Those who were not succumbing to serious mental illness were turning to drink and couldn't shoot straight. Others became twisted sadists and started despatching their victims in 'novel' ways. This, Himmler decided, was no way to run a genocide. He himself had attended a mass execution in Minsk in the late summer of 1941 and almost passed out from the horror — especially when two women captives failed to die from the firing squad and needed to be 'finished off' individually. This he found cruel and upsetting. A better way to kill Jews was what was needed. Something like gassing.

LEFT: A 'panzer-grenadier' fighting in the Russian campaign

OPPOSITE PAGE: Heinrich Himmler talking with SS group leader and Lieutenant General of the Waffen-SS Ritterkreuzträger Eicke, Commander of a division of the Waffen SS

On 20th January 1942, at the Wannsee Conference in Berlin, formal plans were put together by the Nazis for the total elimination of the 11 million Jews thought to be left in Europe. Most would be rounded up into concentration camps and then killed on an industrial scale. The rest would be forced into slave labour and worked until they died. The sites for the first extermination camps (Concentration camps had been around since 1933) had already been decided on in 1941 and experiments with poison gases were well underway. The Germans pressed themselves into action over the next few months, building Treblinka and adding gas chambers to the concentration camp already established at Auschwitz. Before the war had run its course, almost 6 million Jews would be murdered.

GOEBBELS GETS WORRIED

At a meeting with Hitler held in March, Goebbels began to get concerned about the personal health of the Führer, noticing that his hair was turning grey in many places. The Führer revealed to Goebbels that he was fighting off bouts of giddiness. He also confessed, (to Goebbels' concern) to having developed *'a physical revulsion against frost and snow'*. Looking about the room with an intense gaze. He came close to Goebbels and whispered that his greatest torment was that Germany still had snow on the ground…

AN AUSPICIOUS LANDMARK

On 30th March, a German army report showed the Wehrmacht to be in a shocking state. There were 162 German divisions on the Eastern Front, but only eight would be capable of any real offensive action. Between them, the sixteen armoured divisions could muster just 140 tanks in full working order — less than one division. On 30th April 1942, the one millionth German soldier died in combat in the Soviet Union. The invasion was proving far more costly than ever expected and those doing the reckoning might also have worried that the Soviets could still call on far, far more soldiers than Germany ever could. Aware of their shocking losses, German generals were sent off to Hungary and Romania to scrounge up more divisions, while Hitler himself (accompanied by Göring) was forced to turn to Italy cap in hand to beg more troops off Il Duce, promising that the war in Russia would be over by 1942. By the time the Nazi *'charm offensive'* ended, they were assured of 27 Romanian, 13 Hungarian, 9 Italian, 2 Slovak and one Spanish divisions — 42 in total. In private, the Nazis complained bitterly about relying on *'foreign'* divisions.

(By the start of 1943 however, Germany would finally come to realise just how short it still was of troops and would actively consider conscripting the men of the Baltic States into the Wehrmacht to fight for them.)

ABOVE: Soviet child soldiers in the Stalingrad region

DEADLIER THAN THE MALE

One of the main secrets of superior Soviet manpower was, in fact, womanpower. At the start of the conflict, the Soviets were very hesitant to let women take up combat roles, despite their apparent eagerness to volunteer to serve. The huge losses suffered by the Red Army during 1941 changed Stalin's mind.

800,000 women served as part of the Soviet Armed Forces from 1942 until 1945 — and a quarter of them won decorations for their heroism. Predictably many served with medical units, but women could be found in a wide number of other roles as well.

In the Soviet Air Force, initial attempts to sideline women pilots or otherwise protect them from combat were quickly abandoned after devastating initial losses. Three aviation combat regiments were formed, exclusively for women. Not only were the pilots female but so too were all the ground and support staff. The 586th Fighter Aviation Regiment was the first into action, flying its initial combat sorties on 16th April 1942. The Regiment achieved 38 kills and produced two Soviet air aces — Lydia Litvyak (12 kills) and Yekaterina Budanova (11 kills), both flying Yak 1s. The 46th Taman Guards Night Bomber Aviation Regiment gained fame as 'The Night Witches'. This was the Germans' nickname for the women bomber crews flying virtually obsolete Polikarpov Po-2 dive bomber biplanes on daring night raids. The 125th Guards Bomber Aviation Regiment — the third all-female unit — was commanded by the legendary early aviatrix Marina Raskova until she was killed in combat.

On the ground, women officially served as machine gunners, tank crew (Aleksandra Samusenko reached the rank of tank brigade commander), anti-aircraft gunners and snipers. The Red Army's most celebrated female sniper, Lyudmila Pavlichenko, shot and killed over 300 enemy combatants, mainly during the siege of Sevastopol. After being injured, she was sent to America on a publicity tour, where she was serenaded in a song especially written for her by Woodie Guthrie but also publically criticised for both her drab low hemline and for looking fat in her uniform. Two thousand women served as snipers with the Red Army during World War Two. 500 survived. Outside of the Red Army, many thousands more women served with Partisan groups, fighting behind enemy lines throughout occupied territories.

Despite their obvious heroism and outstanding achievements, women soldiers were forbidden to march in the big Moscow Victory Parade in June of 1945. Stalin had decided they needed to be back at home now, breeding a new generation of comrades.

RIGHT: A Female anti-aircraft defence soldier taking observation of the sky

EINSATZGRUPPE D

Assigned to the Southern Ukraine, Einsatzgruppe D murdered 90,000 men, women and children in their area between June 1941 and 1942. They would typically turn up at a town or village and order all Jews to assemble for 'relocation'. They would then be driven out of town, lined up and shot.

In early 1942 however, Himmler sent Einsatzgruppe D fresh orders saying that Jewish women and children were no longer to be shot like their menfolk. Instead he sent them specially adapted vans. Women and children would be loaded into the back of these, ostensibly to be relocated, unaware that the van exhaust fumes were being channelled back inside. Smothered by carbon monoxide fumes, they would drift away and die in their sleep. It was all to be very humane — except the drivers of the vans became progressively more unhinged — and drove their the vans at breakneck speed to get the killing over with. Carbon monoxide fumes would flood into the vans and kill the women and children by suffocation. The drivers also hated having to unload the vans later. Worst of all for Einsatzgruppe D though, the vans could only kill 15-25 women and children at a time, and things were getting way behind schedule.

YOU DONT HAVE TO BE JEWISH....

'In the camps for Russian prisoners, they have begun to eat each other'.

Hermann Göring, October 1941

Out of 5.7 million Soviet soldiers taken prisoner between the launch of Operation Barbarossa in June 1941 and February 1945, 3.3 million died in captivity. Many were sent to camps which were no such thing. Instead they were little more than vast open fields surrounded by rings of barbed wire with no buildings or even tents as shelter. To relieve their boredom, German guards might sometimes take pot shots

RIGHT: Heinrich Himmler

at prisoners behind the wire. Food and water was scarce, if provided at all. The arrival of food — at best chunks of horseflesh — could often start a mass riot as men in a state of starvation tore each other apart to get at the meagre spoils. In places, things became so bad that cannibalism was rife. The weaker prisoners were stalked around the confines of the 'camp', cornered and killed by the stronger ones, and then butchered for their meat. Diseases like typhus claimed further hundreds of thousands.

After the war, German authorities blamed the horrors on being accidentally overwhelmed by the sheer numbers of Soviet troops that surrendered. The implication was that the Russians had brought about their own misery by their cowardice. The truth is that the Germans had always intended to impose mass starvation and slaughter upon the people of the East. Why should POW camps be any different?

INSIDE LENINGRAD

By the start of 1942, as many as 1,000 civilians every day were dying of cold and hunger within the besieged city as temperatures as low as — 30 degrees C took hold. Corpses were a common sight in the streets. Within just a few months, the citizens had killed and eaten their pets and were now reliant on catching rats or birds to supplement their tiny bread ration. Rumours of cannibalism started, the full extent of which is still not known. The NKVD files include a mother smothering and butchering her toddler to keep her three older children alive and a husband who slaughtered his wife to feed their sons. The NKVD used stories of cannibalism within the city to help retain its authority.

Anyone not obeying the state, it declared, would be thrown into a cell full of cannibals and most likely end up being eaten alive. By the end of 1942, the NKVD had officially arrested 2,105 suspected cannibals. Many were shot and the rest imprisoned. 64% of them were women. A far more common crime was civilians killing each other to obtain the victim's ration card.

THE 2ND AND 3RD BATTLES OF KHARKOV

After his overambitious counter-attacks at the start of the year started to falter due to sheer attrition and exhaustion, Stalin was still more than eager to carry on attacking. On 12th May 1942 — just six days before a rival German offensive (Operation Fridericus) was scheduled to commence — he launched the Kharkov Offensive in the southern Ukraine with 640,000 men under Marshal Timoshenko, dubbing it:

'The campaign for the complete and final liberation of the Ukraine against the Nazi invaders'.

It failed. This was partly because — having suffered more than a million casualties during the defence of Moscow — the Red Army was now filled out with hundreds of thousands of raw, untried conscripts being thrown against battle-hardened German veterans. The attack started with a huge artillery bombardment but then advancing Soviet troops found that the Germans had earlier retreated to new defensive lines and were unaffected by the shelling Where those lines were none of the Soviet commanders knew. Their troops kept advancing and advancing into unoccupied territory. It felt like victory. First contact

LEFT: Executions of Jews by German army mobile killing units (Einsatzgruppen) near Ivangorod Ukraine.

MIDDLE: Magirus-Deutz van as used by the Einsatzgruppen

RIGHT: The entrance to the Jewish ghetto in Brody, Western Ukraine

was made with the Germans on the very outskirts of Kharkov. The German lines seemed especially strong — as indeed they were. Unwittingly, the Soviet troops had advanced into an elaborate trap — a trap comprised of a massive German troop build-up which the Soviets had not detected. The Red Army forces were caught in a pincer movement and swiftly surrounded. In the city itself, fierce street fighting broke out between the opposing armour of the German I SS Panzer Corps and the Soviet 3rd Tank Army, reducing whole districts to pulverised burning rubble. For a time, the Soviets even succeeded in driving German armour from Kharkov but were then hit by a massive Nazi counterattack comprising the II SS Panzer Corps as well as the 1st and 4th Panzer Armies. During the fighting, the Germans enjoyed almost total air superiority and used that advantage to the full, being able to call on ten bomber, six fighter and four dive bomber groups. By 18th March, the city was back in German hands.

The battle then played out in a by now familiar way. The Russians did everything they could to break out of the trap and were massacred. A large number of Soviet soldiers attempting to surrender were simply machine gunned. All Jews and political officers caught were executed. Seriously wounded soldiers were denied medical treatment and left to die. By the end of May 1942, the Soviets had lost over 250,000 men. The German soldiers in the field were elated.

TOP LEFT: German artillery, Nebelwerfer PK 670

LEFT: Marshall Semyon Konstantinovich Timoshenko

RIGHT: German soldiers in the outposts of the Kharkov area, May 1942

PQ13

A British arctic supply convoy designed PQ13 set sail for Russia on March 20th but this time German U-Boats were waiting for it — and five of the 19 merchant ships and escorts were lost. For the survivors of the stricken ships forced into the arctic waters, there was next to no hope of survival.

THE NEW CRIMEAN WAR

Down south on the Black Sea, von Manstein finally decided to seek revenge on the Soviet forces who had stopped him from seizing Sevastopol last December. Operation Bustard, launched on 11th May, saw a major German offensive against Soviet troops and facilities on the Kerch Peninsula to the east of Crimea. He was also supplied with 32 gigantic siege guns to be turned on the fortress city of Sevastopol and to crack it open once and for all. By 15th May the Kerch Peninsula was in German hands and Sevastopol completely surrounded.

On 2nd June, 600 heavy guns launched a furious barrage against Sevastopol. The barrage would last five whole days. On the 6th, the Luftwaffe were called to join in and blitz Sevastopol and then — having notionally softened up the city — von Manstein's 11th Army began their ground assault at 2.30 am on 7th June. They were joined on the 11th by the Romanian Mountain Corps and 30th Army Corps. They were met, blow for blow, by the 180,000 strong garrison of Russian soldiers defending the city. Von Manstein's attack sputtered to an awkward halt on 16th June as Axis forces were successfully repulsed. Von Manstein rapidly reordered and rallied his troops and launched a fresh offensive the following day. Ten days later, the Germans and their Romanian allies had succeeded in capturing a number of important hilltop positions around the city, but had not managed to break into the city itself. That all changed on 30th June when the order was given to evacuate the city with the help of the Russian Black Sea Fleet. As the defenders tried to escape, Axis forces streamed into the

ARMS FOR RUSSIA . . . A great convoy of British ships escorted by Soviet fighter planes sails into Murmansk harbour with vital supplies for the Red Army.

LEFT: Arms for Russia poster- a great convoy of British ships escorted by Soviet fighters sails into Murmansk harbour with vital supplies for the Red Army.

ABOVE: Sevastopol in Crimea , three German soldiers drag a wounded soldier to safety

To 7 July   To 22 July   To 1 August   To 18 November

breach and swiftly secured a number of strategic positions throughout the fallen city. By 2nd July, Sevastopol was officially in German hands, along with some 90,000 Soviet prisoners who had not been fortunate enough to get on a ship to safety.

OPERATION BLUE

After the Soviets had lost so many men in the Ukraine in their early year campaigns, Hitler very quickly decided to take full advantage of the situation by launching his own offensive — Operation Blue. This was intended to secure the Don and Volga rivers then seize Russia's oil production facilities, by crossing the Caucasus mountains and driving to the very edge of the Caspian Sea.

However Hitler saw the city of Stalingrad as a major prize too. It was a major centre of industry, communications and transport for the Russians. The city itself was around 25 miles long, stretched along the River Volga to its back, and at around 3 miles deep the Volga was a vital supply route running north to Moscow and by blocking it Hitler could start to deprive the north of essential war supplies including most especially oil.

The seizure of the oil fields — and the capture of Stalingrad. Hitler wanted them both, and he wanted them both now, Many of Hitler's commanders felt a real sense of unease at the Führer's plans. There simply weren't enough men, tanks and supplies to attack in two different offensives — let alone enough reserves to be held in support. When Halder personally raised concerns about the lack of materials to support twin offensives, he and his brother officers were told the Russians were finished and then subjected to a tirade of abuse from the Führer both for being useless officers and for lacking imagination. (After the war, Halder recorded an event that illustrated well the Führer's state of mind. Presented with an army report that concluded that the Red Army could still gather between one million and one million fresh troops in the northern Stalingrad area, half a million more men from the Caucasus as well as 1200 fresh tanks coming off the Production line each month., Hitler *'flew at the man who was reading with clenched fists and foam in the corners of his mouth and forbade him to read any more of such idiotic twaddle'*.)

Nevertheless, the Führer's will prevailed. The available forces would be split and the 6th Army would be despatched off to seize Stalingrad (later to be joined by the 4th Panzer Army).

Stalin was utterly baffled and confused by the Nazi plan as details of the

RIGHT: A German Army armoured unit heading to the Volga after passing the Don River. Russia, July 1942

German's movement started to come in from 28th June onwards. He had been certain that Hitler would drive on to Moscow in the summer of 1942 and was caught out now by this sudden emphasis on the south. He had no good plans to offer for resistance except to fall back on the old insistence on no retreats.

A RACE PUZZLE

Hitler moved to a new field headquarters situated near the town of Vinnitsa in the Ukraine in July 1942, better to direct Army Groups A and B as they advanced towards their separate objectives.

Martin Bormann accompanied him as his secretary and was immediately shocked at the appearance of Ukrainian children. Rather than being bestial and sub human, they looked remarkably like the Aryan children the Reich had promoted as superior. Some were even blonde and blue eyed. Rather than accept that his racial theories were flawed, Bormann was forced to conclude that the filthy lifestyles that the Ukrainian subhumans indulged in had meant that only the strongest could possibly survive. That was why the very strongest and best now looked racially superior.

HITLER CHANGES HIS MIND

By the end of July, the German offensive was going exceptionally well in the drive for the oilfields, which were now just a few hundred kilometres away. The weather was good, the troops in shorts and rolled-up shirt sleeves were singing army songs and the Panzers had entered Rostov and reached the bridge over the River Don. The Soviets, on the other hand, had lost 83,000 POWs to the Germans and were otherwise busy shooting their own fleeing troops.

Despite this, in his new HQ in Vinnitsa, Hitler was proving increasingly irascible. He hated being somewhere foreign and he hated the summer heat. Although he would never admit it, he was also unsure.

The capture of Rostov by Army Group A had put the Germans in a very favourable position to drive on to the Caucasus oilfields, but then abruptly Hitler fatally weakened them by sending the 4th Panzer Army first to support the oilfields offensive then changed his mind and sent them back 300 miles away to support efforts around Stalingrad. He also deprived them of vital artillery which he then had sent up all the way north to use against Leningrad — which still stood proud despite his express wishes and manifest will.

Army Group A, now fatally weakened, drove on to the oilfields but could not muster the sheer firepower it needed. They simply could not fight their way past Malgobek and on to the strategically vital Grozny.

At the start of September, when Army Group A fighting in the Caucasus appeared to lose some momentum, its commander Field Marshal List was personally removed by Hitler. Having no one else he trusted or thought was up to the job, Hitler then appointed himself as the new head of Army Group A. Later that same month, he fired Halder and appointed in his place the most obsequious commander he could find. Halder was, in the Führer's own words *'no longer equal to the psychic demands of his position'*. Whatever that meant, he carried on by saying that what he needed now were passionate Nazis and not professional soldiers. (Halder would subsequently be arrested and imprisoned in Dachau. He survived the war to be liberated by the Americans on 28th April 1945.) When Halder's fellow general, Jodl attempted to come to Halder's defence, Hitler retaliated by refusing to shake hands or dine in the same room as him for several months.

STALIN CHANGES HIS MIND

Something happened to Josef Stalin's military thinking as the Germans advanced that summer. In the space of just weeks he changed his thinking from shooting any comrade who retreated to accepting the idea of *'a fighting retreat'*. The concept worked. Empowered and given greater mobility, Soviet forces often proved deft enough to slip out of the way of encircling German units and fall back to fight again. They were no longer getting surrounded, cut off and massacred as they had so many times before. The Germans now had to chase them harder — stretching their supply lines. At the same time, Soviet hit and run tactics started to wear down their opponent's forces.

THE FIGHT FOR LENINGRAD

In late August 1942, both the German Army Group North and Soviet forces in the vicinity of Leningrad launched operations to either take or relieve the city. Although the Soviets suffered especially heavy casualties in the fighting, neither side gained a commanding upper hand. The German offensive was halted but the city was not relieved and its suffering would continue.

STALINGRAD

By mid-August German armour with General Friedrich von Paulus's 6th Army was within sight of Stalingrad. Assigned to the task of conquering it were 270,000 men, 500 Panzers and 1600 fighters and bombers. Prior to their arrival, the city had been subjected to a furious bombardment by the Luftwaffe to soften it up — and 40,000 civilians were already dead in the ruins.

Now, Paulus's forces surrounded the city on three sides, with the Volga at the back of the defending Soviets. The Battle for Stalingrad had begun. German troops poured into the city on 13th September, trapping thousands of civilians in their homes and fighting their way through the through vast industrial estates and into the city streets. As the Soviets tried to rush troops and supplies to the front across the Volga by boat, they were preyed upon by Ju 87 Stuka dive bombers. They were more successful than the German panzers heading for the river, who found manoeuvring in the city difficult and all-too-often fell prey to handfuls of Soviet troops assigned the task of tank killing. Infantry, it quickly became obvious, would be the deciding factor in the city.

In charge of the 62nd Army defending the city was the Soviet commander Vasily Chuikov. Where his German counterpart von Paulus was calm, measured and even gentle, Chuikov was a famed bully, a street thug with abundant energy who both terrified and galvanised the officers and men under his command. He would arrest 13,000 men under his own command during the battle of Stalingrad — and summarily execute many of them.

As the city rapidly became reduced to pulverised ruins (not one building

LEFT: General of Panzer Troops Paulus (right), northern part of Stalingrad

MIDDLE: Stalingrad, PK 694 gun emplacement

RIGHT: Soldiers take food to the infantry in the conquered gun factory in Stalingrad

in the city was said to be undamaged), Chuikov developed new tactics for street fighting, insisting that his lines should ideally be no more than a grenade toss from the enemy. That way, the Germans would not dare to bring their artillery to bear or use the Luftwaffe for ground support. It was a tactic the Viet Cong and NVA would later adopt in Vietnam.

The battle in the ruins soon degenerated into house to house fighting with small arms, grenades, knives and even entrenching tools being the weapons of choice. The Germans, used to freewheeling, fast-moving Blitzkrieg tactics, were not adequately prepared for street fighting and did not understand it (or relish it) in the way that their enemies did. Chuikov himself observed:

'The Germans could not stand close fighting; they opened up with their automatic weapons from well over half a mile away…They could not bear us to come close to them…'

In mid-September, a determined German push saw them reach and seize the city's main railway station. Soviet forces sent to recapture it suffered 90% losses — but achieved their objective. In just six hours, the station changed hands no less than 14 times.

The opposing lines ebbed and flowed. At one point the Germans were little more than 300 metres from the banks of the River Volga, with the Russians desperately holding out in a small enclave but fighting with an almost insane determination. At this point in the battle, the life expectancy of a new Soviet soldier shipped into the conflict across the Volga was just 24 hours. As the advance ground to a halt once more, snipers made further movement almost impossible — and there were many more Soviet snipers than German ones. The Germans generally considered sniping unmanly.

LEFT: Battle of Stalingrad – German infantrymen in position

MIDDLE: German soldiers of the 24th Panzer Division in action in the southern station of Stalingrad

RIGHT: Stalingrad, German infantry foxhole covered by the wreck of a Russian tank T 34

TOP RIGHT: General Friedrich Paulus

The Soviets on the other hand feted their snipers as national heroes. Observing that the Germans also preferred to fight by day, Chuikov decided that the night would belong to him, launching raids under cover of darkness to retrieve territory ceded to the Reich during daylight hours. It worked.

Within just two months, the Germans in the city had suffered enormous casualties — but reinforcing them proved difficult. Inexperienced soldiers rushed to the front line had little grasp of how to fight amongst ruins — or how to survive. They were sniper fodder. Unnerved as they were by the snipers, German troops were more in fear of the Soviet snatch squads, sent across no-man's-land or through the sewers to take prisoners for interrogation. No one doubted their fate should they be unlucky enough to be captured. They would be *'washed'* — a term coined by the Soviets for a combination of severe torture and a beating. They would then be shot.

Given the ferocity and intensity of the continued fighting von Paulus had decided to concentrate the German forces available within the city and leave his flanks guarded by those he considered inferior — chiefly Hungarian

and Romanian units. It was to prove a costly mistake. Nevertheless, by November 1942, the Germans could claim they held 90% of the city. On the banks of the Volga, the Russians dug in with more and more determination. Their main HQ was constructed underground, and other field commands used the sewers as their base.

THE POINTLESSNESS OF STALINGRAD

Military historians have noted that — although it changed the course of the war — the battle of Stalingrad was actually tactically pointless. Germany simply didn't need to win the city. German forces had already seized control of the River Volga and its trade routes at strategic positions both north and south of Stalingrad. The blockade was already tight and underway. The true motivation for the ongoing effort to take Stalingrad was Hitler's personal pride — and a seething, spiteful, personal determination to destroy something that began with *'Stalin...'*

ABOVE: German sniper using the Mauser 98k rifle with Russian PE scope mounted. This set-up was unusual but local German Waffenmeisters (amourers) of infantry battalions, did mount captured Russian optics to the standard German 98k

THE ARCTIC CONVOYS RESUME

British supply convoys to Russia resumed on 2nd December 1942, after the merchant navy vessels were freed up from urgent duties in the Mediterranean supporting the North African campaign. Convoy PQ18 comprised some 40 ships with an escort of 17 Royal Navy destroyers as well as the aircraft carrier HMS Avenger. By the time it arrived in the Soviet Union on 26th September, it had lost 13 ships to bitter enemy action.

STARVATION IN KHARKOV

In the winter of 1942, famine broke out in the southern Ukrainian city of Kharkov. While the city's German military administration requisitioned enough food for German troops in the area as well as meagre rations for the essential civilian forced labourers, everyone else was considered completely expendable. They were unnutzer esser ('a useless eater').

The elderly and children starved and died first. Survivors from the city reported that people were first reduced to killing and butchering pets before trying to hunt down vermin like rats and pigeons to survive. Even the rats seemed to run out. Some people, in desperation, began to dig up the recently deceased from their graves. Others gnawed at the bark of trees in the city parks or consumed grass, leaves and twigs. During the time of starvation, the German authorities deliberately sealed the town to prevent the inhabitants from foraging in the countryside. Anyone caught trying to leave was shot.

By the time the famine had ended, in the early months of 1943, perhaps as many as 100,000 of Kharkov's population were dead.

OPERATION URANUS

On 23rd September, the new Chief of the Army General Staff, General Zeitzler assured Hitler that the Soviets were *'in no position to mount a major objective'*. He was wrong. Once again, German intelligence had been sorely lacking. Completely unknown to the Germans, the Soviets under Zhukov had managed to assemble more than a million troops and a vast force of tanks to threaten the 6th Army at Stalingrad.

Operation Uranus was launched in deep snow

ABOVE: German Soldiers taking away food robbed off the local population in Kharkhov region

OPPOSITE PAGE: General Kurt Zeitzler

ABOVE: Battle of Stalingrad during the fall of 1942

early in the morning of 19th November 1942 with a concentrated 500 gun barrage. Soviet commanders had learned enough to use Germany's own Blitzkrieg tactics against them, attacking a narrow area with speed and ferocity to break the enemy line. Zhukov concentrated on the Romanian units guarding the Germans within the city to the north — and crushed them utterly within a day. On the 20th, he hit the Romanians to the south and broke their lines with terrifying speed. The two attacking forces to north and south joined up at Kalach on the 22nd, trapping some 300,000 Axis soldiers in almost indefensible last ditch pockets.

General Zeitzler was now quick to change his mind and advised Hitler to let the 6th Army perform a fighting retreat before they were completely trapped. In response, he was subjected to a tirade of abuse. *'Where the German soldier sets foot, there he remains!'* Hitler shrieked. When the Führer was not present, other senior officers literally begged Zeitzler to order the retreat anyway, but he would not go against Hitler. Instead, he went on a personal stubborn little hunger strike in solidarity with his men fighting in Stalingrad. He lost 26lbs in just two weeks and might possibly have died had not Bormann informed on him to Hitler, who gave him orders to stop being so stupid forthwith.

In Stalingrad, Paulus too saw the danger but his reactions were slowed by having to consult Hitler in person before taking any significant action. The units he did send against the Russians almost immediately experienced mobility problems due to the cold and snow and poor visibility. The German 6th Army were effectively encircled within just five days — cut off, without supplies and quickly consuming their own food resources. They would very soon have next to nothing to eat.

Initially, the Germans within Stalingrad were not unduly alarmed. They considered the Soviet forces deeply inferior in almost every way and were certain that the Führer would send forces to relieve them in just a matter of days.

Hitler hunched over the map tables and told Paulus to stay put and make no attempt to break out. Göring had reassured him that the 6th Army could be resupplied from the air by his Luftwaffe. This was a nonsense. Trapped inside Stalingrad now were 20 German divisions and a further two Romanian divisions. They would require the very minimum of 750 tons of supplies to be delivered each and every day — a task far, far beyond the wildest dreams of the Luftwaffe. At the same time, Hitler instructed Field Marshal von Manstein to assault the Soviet blockade and punch through it to relieve Paulus in the city.

OPERATION WINTER TEMPEST

Von Manstein began his assault with the 4th Panzer Army and grave doubts on 12th December, in an operation codenamed Winter Tempest. It was doomed to failure. There were 60 Soviet divisions between his tanks and the trapped 6th Army. He had asked Hitler to order the 6th to fight their way out of the city to join up with his relief force, but the Führer insisted that German soldiers did not retreat and that von Manstein needed to travel the entire distance to where von Paulus was defending.

By 19th December, the Germans had fought their way closer than 50km from Stalingrad and the trapped 6th could actually see their flares at night. Von Manstein sent orders to Paulus to disobey the Führer and attempt a break out. Paulus, a loyal soldier, hesitated, and the moment was lost. Shortly after, the 4th Panzer army themselves had to beat a hasty and ungainly retreat in order to prevent themselves becoming trapped and encircled by the superior Soviet forces.

At the same time, Göring's plans to supply the 6th Army by air were also proving hopeless. Many of the supplies dropped by parachute would drift behind Soviet lines — the opposing forces were just too close to each other to drop with any precision.

Huddled in whatever shelter they could find, tormented by — 30 degree temperatures and ever fearful of Soviet snipers or, the German soldiers in the city began to realise just how much trouble they were in. On Christmas Day 1942, they held what celebrations they could — and as the sound of Stille Nacht drifted through the frigid air, a number of officers took the opportunity of the distraction to slip away and shoot themselves.

ABOVE LEFT: Soviet soldiers fight off the roof of a house in Stalingrad

ABOVE RIGHT: Improvised Winter boots

RIGHT: Soviet Soldiers clear buildings in Stalingrad

1943

CASABLANCA

Josef Stalin did not attend the Allied summit in Casablanca that was held in January 1943. He had suddenly developed a deep fear of being deposed in his absence, perhaps by his own military or perhaps by other indefinable *'shadowy forces'*. Instead he stayed at home and fumed that the Allies had still not opened the *'Second Front'* to the west to do their share of the fighting. He growled that the Allies were trying to distract him with trivial issues of ongoing war supplies instead of dealing with the pressing need for war in the west complaining:

'Hundreds of thousands of Soviet people are giving their lives in the struggle against fascism, and Churchill is haggling with us about two dozen Hurricanes. And anyway those Hurricanes are crap...'

ANOTHER FIGHT FOR LENINGRAD

On 12th January 1943 , the Soviets launched Operation Spark in another utterly desperate bid to break the siege of Leningrad. The Leningrad and Volkhov Fronts of the Red Army turned on the well-fortified German positions south of Lake Lagoda and in less than a week managed to force a 10-12 km corridor through to the city. It wasn't much — but it was something.

THE FALL OF STALINGRAD

'Surrender is forbidden. Sixth Army will hold their positions to the last man and the last round and by their heroic endurance will make an unforgettable contribution toward the establishment of a defensive front and the salvation of the Western world'

Hitler's orders to von Paulus, Stalingrad 25th January 1943.

ABOVE: Soviet propaganda poster "Beat the German beasts! The destruction of Hitler's army is possible and necessary" 1943

To 12 December　　To 18 February　　To March (Soviet Advance Only)

As `1942 turned into 1943, the plight of the German forces surrounded in Stalingrad grew rapidly worse. On Friday 8th January, the Soviets offered the beleaguered 6th Army terms for their formal surrender. They were rebuffed.

On 10th January, the Soviets subjected the 6th to a massive artillery bombardment with thousands of artillery pieces and Katyusha rocket launchers all trained on the German positions. The same day, the Soviets launched Operation Ring to further squeeze and shrink enemy lines. By now, everyone it seemed was talking about suicide. It was no longer the prerogative of officers. On the last makeshift airfields inside the city, those soldiers who preferred the option of escape pursued the few transport aircraft still operational. They clung to their icy wings or undercarriage in desperation as the planes took off. Inevitably, they would lose their grip and fall to their deaths. On 28th January, all that was left of the once mighty 6th was three small pockets of resistance. Von Paulus was reduced to commanding what he could from the basement of a famous department store.

Hitler promoted von Paulus to Field Marshal on 30th January. With the promotion came a snide reminder that no German field marshal had ever surrendered. The implication was clear. Hitler now expected von Paulus to kill himself. Von Paulus however had different ideas. He was a Christian and thought suicide a sin. A day later he surrendered to Russian forces. When he received the news, Hitler was both beside himself with rage and utterly baffled, calling his newest field marshal a *'characterless weakling'.* Paulus could have gone into immortality, he told his high command. Instead, for some reason, he chose to go to Moscow instead.

Paulus's journey to Moscow was by all accounts a comfortable — even luxurious — one and he survived the war. His men were not so lucky. 90,000 Germans were captured at Stalingrad. Of those, 95% of the ordinary soldiers and their NCOs would not survive captivity. 95% of the senior German officers who were captured survived. They included no less than 24 Generals. 40,000 civilians were killed during the fighting and the Red army took in excess of 650,000 casualties.

THE NEWS BREAKS

There was no hiding the fate of the German 6th Army from the people back home in Germany it was decided. Instead an official announcement simply said:

'The battle of Stalingrad has ended. True to their oath to fight to the last breath, the Sixth Army under the exemplary leadership of

RIGHT: Soviet soldier waving the Red Banner over the central plaza of Stalingrad

Field Marshal Paulus has been overcome by the superiority of the enemy and by the unfavourable circumstances confronting our forces'.

The announcement on radio was preceded by martial drums and followed up by some Beethoven. Four days of national mourning were declared and all theatres and cinemas shut down. It was a shattering blow to German morale. Minister of Propaganda Goebbels responded by calling for the entire German nation to offer itself for 'Total War'. Sacrifices would have to be made and deprivations would have to be endured. Civilians would go without so that what Germany had could all be devoted to the war effort.

MORE FAILURE IN THE SOUTH

Stalingrad was not the only defeat Hitler had to endure in early 1943. The Soviets were busy elsewhere too and in response to the threat — and the strategically disastrous loss of Stalingrad, Hitler reluctantly allowed the 12th Panzer Army from Army Group A to be withdrawn from the Caucasus and retreat hundreds of kilometres back through Rostov after Zeitzler warned him, *'unless you order a withdrawal from the Caucasus now, we shall soon have a second Stalingrad on our hands'.* .

The forces in the Caucasus had achieved relatively little anyway. They had reached and seized some of the northernmost of the Soviet oilfields, only to find that the retreating Russians had already destroyed them. They had also struggled with some degree of futility to get any further south, failing to find mountain passes that could be successfully traversed or assaulted. The rest of Army Group A had to fall back too, ferociously harried by advancing Soviet forces. By March of 1943, they needed to be saved by air support.

Flushed with success at the epic victory at Stalingrad, the Soviets now swept from the River Don to the West of Stalingrad, retook the city of Kursk on 8th February and then Kharkov on 16th February. Von Manstein counter attacked, using a specially trained SS Panzer Corps riding Tiger tanks on 20th February, retaking Kharkov once more in mid to late March. It was a typical outcome. The Soviets launched no less than eight winter offensives during this period, only to have them blunted and rolled back by the Germans. Their success in dealing with the Soviet attacks gave the Germans a false sense of security and perhaps even reckless boldness. Manstein and Hitler then turned their gaze on a seemingly vulnerable Soviet salient one hundred miles deep and 150 miles wide at a place called Kursk.

OPERATION CITADEL

After the fall of Stalingrad and the retreat from the Caucasus, the German High Command still did not fully realise that they had now effectively lost the war. Instead, they saw what they thought was an excellent opportunity to strike back by taking the Kursk salient, a bulge in the enemy lines that looked particularly vulnerable to encirclement. Hitler sounded excited at the opportunity saying *'The victory at Kursk must shine like a beacon to the world'*. Behind the scenes he was now nervous and hesitant. He understood what it would mean if the dice fell unkindly for him this time. Now it was the generals who were persuading him, assuring him that Soviet manpower was depleted almost to the point of complete exsanguination. All the good troops were dead. All Stalin could call on were the dregs of the country bumpkins. Hitler — reluctantly — agreed. He liked the idea of revenge — these were the same soldiers who had beaten him at Stalingrad and had forced him from the Caucasus — and a victory here could see German control of both the Don and the Volga once more. Unfortunately for the Reich, German intelligence was as wrong as ever — and the Soviets had waged an excellent campaign of misinformation behind the scenes.

General von Kluge would attack from the north with the entire 9th Army and von Manstein from the south spearheaded by the 4th Panzer Army and accompanied by the II SS Panzer Corps and divisions of the Großdeutschland Panzergrenadiers — a classic German pincer movement. Taking part in the assault would be almost 800,000 soldiers, 3000 panzers, 10,000 artillery pieces and in excess of 2,000 Luftwaffe fighters and bombers. Facing them, the Soviets were rapidly mustering almost 1,500,000 troops, over 5000 tanks, 25,000 heavy guns and nearly 3000 warplanes.

Unfortunately for the Germans, preparations to take Kursk suffered a string of disastrous delays. Men and supplies were slow in assembling and it proved exceptionally difficult to both acquire and wrangle the new Ferdinand (Later Elefant) heavy tank hunter with 88mm gun that was thought to be essential to the campaign. This gave the Soviets more than enough time to prepare for the German onslaught, with vast minefields comprising over 1 million mines, improved fighting positions, sweeping fields of tank traps, and 3,000 miles of trenchlines defended by greatly increased troop numbers. The Germans finally attacked on 5th July.

Zhukov let the Germans come on in, expending fuel and ammunition whilst dashing themselves against the excellently prepared defences and exposing themselves to ferocious attacks from Il-2 Sturmovik dive bombers. The German 9th Army to the north found it particularly hard going and two separate offensives failed in short order. The southern thrust penetrated twice as deeply, but could still not achieve a decisive breakthrough. After a week, he struck back against the bloodied, battered and exhausted Germans with largely fresh armour and men. German armour found itself up against the new SU 122 — which boasted a massive 122mm gun on a T-34 Chassis and the SU 152 with an even more powerful 152mm. On the German side, the Ferdinand proved itself to be a very effective tank killer — when it could be brought to bear and when it didn't break down. Both were capable of stopping anything. Kursk proved to be the largest single tank battle the world had ever known. On one day alone — 12th July —

ABOVE: General Günther von Kluge & Adolf Hitler

ABOVE: Northwest of Stalingrad, tank borne infantry leap from their carriers to attack the Nazi troops now on the defensive.

over 1,000 tanks fought a pitched battle close to the town of Pokrovka.

By 13th July the Germans were in full retreat having lost over 500,000 men and 1,000 panzers. Hitler agreed with the decision to retreat, having lost his nerve now, but to save face he told the generals that it was simply to preserve men and armour to reinforce Italy now that the Allies had invaded Sicily. He also took direct command over everything military. The generals, he reasoned, could no longer be trusted to win. In doing this he proved that he simply had no idea of what he had come up against. At Kursk, Soviet losses were twice those of Hitler's own forces, but they still won the battle. The Soviet Union could take a level of punishment which the Third Reich simply couldn't endure and had reserves of men and materials to call upon and then send into battle that the Wehrmacht could only ever dream of.

GO WEST

Following the epic events at Kursk, the Soviets began to roll west in a series of thunderous counteroffensives. From now on, there would simply be no stopping them. German forces were unable to blunt the assault. They fell back out of their Orel salient and the Soviets swept in on 5th August. Further south, determined Soviet forces punched through Army Group South's positions in Bryansk and headed for Kharkov once more. Despite ferocious battles between Tigers and Soviet armour, the Russians proved just more manoeuvrable and an outflanked panzer force was compelled to retreat. All Germans had evacuated Kharkov again by 22nd August. It would never again fall into their hands.

The 1st Panzer Army and a partially-reconstructed 6th Army located on the River Mius were just too weak to hold back a determined Soviet assault and had to fall back fast, abandoning vast swathes of captured industry and farmland. Hitler ordered Axis forces to hold and fight at the Dnieper Line — but the fortifications planned for the line were well behind schedule and there was just no time for their completion. The Soviets were too close in pursuit and hard on the heels of the Germans as they crossed the Dnieper. Before effective defensive positions could be established, Russian advanced units were already across the river and well dug in, despite the failure of a large scale Soviet paratrooper drop. In September, Smolensk was retaken and by October, the Germans began to realise that any in-depth defence of the Dnieper Line was just not feasible. They began to fall back once more as Soviet forces took one strategically important town after another. In early November, Soviet forces finally retook Kiev.

West of Kiev, the 4th Panzer Army fought on, holding on to Zhytomyr while elements of Army Group South recaptured Korosten — only to lose it again on Christmas Eve when assaulted by the 1st Ukrainian Front whom they had, quite typically already written off as a spent force.

ABOVE: Soviet soldiers with an anti-tank gun repelling a tank attack during the battle of Kursk

RACE WAR SOVIET STYLE

As the Soviets moved west and started to regain territory, Stalin decided to enact a terrible revenge on some of the minority ethnic populations that he believed had collaborated with their German occupiers. No attempt was made to find guilty individuals, the races would suffer as a whole. These would include the Kalmyks (Mongols by ethnic definition), who lived on the steppes south of Stalingrad. The Kalmyks, Stalin decided, would be relocated to Siberia. They were rounded up at gunpoint en masse in late December 1943 and despatched east by train. It's thought that as many as 50% of the people died on the journey. Those who survived were put to work in forced labour camps and given barely starvation level rations. Many more died in just a matter of weeks. Other ethnic groups, including the Chechens, Tartars, Balkars and Karachai suffered a similar fate.

ABOVE: A tribe of Kalmyk people move to new pastures

REAPING THE WHIRLWIND

It cannot go without mention that at home, Germany was now suffering mightily from the effects of sustained Anglo-American bombing raids on their cities. The Americans would bomb by day, the RAF by night. Giving a lecture to the Nazi gauleiters on 7th November, General Jodl made an interesting comment. He said:

'The war has assumed forms solely through the fault of England such as were believed to be no longer possible since the days of the racial and religious wars'.

It must surely have slipped the good general's mind that this was precisely the sort of war Hitler had announced he would be waging. And in blaming *'England'* for adding atrocity to the conflict, he must too have forgotten the Blitz, and the the Einsatzgruppen.

General Jodl was hung for war crimes on 16th October 1946.

THOUGHTS OF PEACE

By September 1943, Goebbels could see the writing on the wall and was desperately trying to think of a way out. The war was lost. He plucked up courage and talked to Hitler about it in private. He found that the Führer had already given it some thought and actually told Goebbels he *'yearned'* for peace. Goebbels favoured trying to negotiate peace with Stalin, because the Soviet dictator was a pragmatist and Churchill a romantic. Hitler, on the other hand, favoured reaching a deal with the West. He believed that Churchill would see what a threat to the world Stalin was and that the Russian Bear would need to be shot. Strangely, this is very nearly what happened.

A WARMER WINTER

The winter of 1943/44 completely threw the Germans as it was relatively warm. Instead of snow, the Germans now found themselves fighting in deep, treacherous sucking mud. It didn't bother the Soviets. They were equally used to both and their equipment designed to work in both conditions.

ABOVE: General Alfred Jodl

LEFT: Ukrainian troops of the Russian Army moving through thick mud on the Eastern Front

TEHRAN

In November, Josef Stalin did join Roosevelt and Churchill for a grand Allied summit in Tehran. It was the first time the American president had met Stalin and the two men got on better than expected. Churchill was positively alarmed that their war aims seemed to have much in common and actually left the room when the two leaders started making unsavoury jokes about German officers being mass murdered after the war was won. Churchill was frankly frightened about the prospects of any D-Day succeeding without unacceptable Allied casualties and now his American ally seemed very vulnerable to Stalin's forceful demands for a second front. Churchill felt himself being edged out. The leadership of the Allies was rapidly becoming a triumvirate of two.

(Stalin for his part had his fellow leader's rooms bugged and every morning would receive fresh transcripts from his secret police of what they were saying in private.)

An unnerved Churchill later wrote of the occasion:

'There I sat with the great Russian bear on one side of me, with paws outstretched, and on the other side the great American buffalo, and between the two sat the poor little English donkey who was the only one...who knew the right way home.'

After the summit, Churchill's thoughts kept returning to Stalin, with ever-increasing unease. Looking forward, he saw terrible danger from the Soviets. He warned the Americans of *'bloody consequences in the future...Stalin is an unnatural man. There will be grave troubles.'* In May 1944, he wrote to Anthony Eden; *'The Russians are drunk with victory, and there is no length they may not go.'*

Churchill was now only too aware that, in helping Stalin against Hitler, they were merely attacking a vile present day enemy whilst supporting and emboldening an equally vile future foe.

ABOVE: The the first meeting of Stalin, Roosevelt & Churchill at the Tehran conference

OPPOSITE PAGE: Soviet poster 'The Big Three will tie the enemy in knots'. Poster by Kukryniksy

1944

FAMILIAR FRONTIERS

By 3rd January 1944, advance Soviet forces had battled their way west as far as the old 1939 Polish-Soviet border. The following week, elements of those northern forces swept south to join up with Soviet forces moving north from the Dnieper region, in the process surrounding ten German divisions at Korsun— Shevchenkovsky. Hitler meanwhile still irrationally insisted on trying to hold the Dnieper Line even though it had been deeply and permanently compromised and refused to entertain the idea of anything but fighting on and holding ground. Von Manstein virtually ignored him when ordering a break out from what became known as the Cherkassy pocket and in so doing saved significant numbers of troops and armour. The escape was successful but not without casualties. A third of the trapped Germans were killed or captured in the two week action.

One final move in the south completed the 1943—44 campaigning season, which had seen a Soviet advance of over 500 miles. In March 1944, 20 German divisions of Generaloberst Hans-Valentin Hube's 1st Panzer Army were encircled in what was to be known as Hube's Pocket near Kamenets-Podolskiy. After two weeks' of heavy fighting, the 1st Panzer managed to escape the pocket, suffering only light to moderate casualties. At this point, Hitler sacked several prominent generals, von Manstein included. In April, the Red Army took back Odessa, followed by 4th Ukrainian Front's campaign to restore control over the Crimea, which culminated in the recapture of Sevastopol on 10 May.

RIGHT: Propaganda poster by Victor Ivanov: 'You have given us a new lease of life'

ТЫ ВЕРНУЛ НАМ ЖИЗНЬ!

To 1 December To 30 April To 19 August To 31 December

WAR IN THE BALTIC

Army Group North had seen relatively little fighting in 1943 but, in January 1944, they were suddenly on the receiving end of a Soviet Blitzkrieg, courtesy of the Volkhov and Second Baltic Fronts. They were hurled away from both Leningrad and Novgorod and forced to fall back some 75 miles until their Soviet pursuers reached the border of Estonia. Moving into Estonia proved more difficult however as the Germans made good use of Estonian volunteers who were prepared to fight ferociously to keep their homeland from being once again enveloped by the Russians. The advance on the Estonian capital and major seaport was halted in February 1944.

THE RELIEF OF LENINGRAD

The city of Leningrad was finally relieved by the Leningrad and Volkhov Fronts, working in conjunction with the 1st and 2nd Baltic Fronts on 27th January 1944. Aircraft supplied by the Soviet Baltic Fleet provided valuable air support. An estimated 200,000 civilians had been killed by the German heavy guns and other artillery during the course of the siege, and a further 630,000 had succumbed to cold and hunger.

HUNGARY

The Germans took full control of Hungary — their former Axis ally — in March 1944, fearing that the nation would either make peace with the Soviets or switch sides entirely. Until then, Hungary had been a relative safe place for Jews, as the nation had refused to obey German orders and to turn them over to the Nazis. Now things changed with terrifying speed. Adolf Eichmann took personal charge to ensure that the Jewish population was rounded up and deported to the death camps faster than ever seen before. In just 10 days, 116,000 Jewish men, women and children were sent to Auschwitz. In all 440,000 Hungarian Jews would be rounded up and sent to concentration camps. 150,000 would survive. So many Hungarian Jews were killed in so short a space of time that gas supplies ran low.

ABOVE: Otto Adolf Eichmann

LEFT: Auschwitz, Hungarian women who have been selected to work at Auschwitz-Birkenau. June, 1944. Their heads have been shaved to control the lice that spreads typhus. The woman on the left is an auxiliary guard who assists the SS

ABOVE: Soviet sapper cuts through barbed wire

TOP RIGHT: Map showing the position of the VKT-line

SPRING

In March 1944, the Soviets launched a triple thrust south of Krivoi Rog, at Uman and at Shepetovka. In six weeks they fought the Germans back some 160 miles. Meanwhile by May, Soviet forces had cleared the last of the Germans out of the Crimean peninsula.

THE COLLAPSE OF THE AXIS ALLIANCE

Soviet troops advanced into Romania in April, attempting nothing less than an invasion of the country. Their first invasion attempt (the First Jassy-Kishinev Offensive) began on 8th April but had failed by 6th June. The Second Jassy-Kishinev Offensive, waged between 20th August and 29th August, proved far more effective and decisive. August saw the destruction of German forces at Kishinev and the capture of the Romanian Ploesti oil fields. Romania switched sides during the fighting by virtue of a coup and the reconstituted German 6th Army was trapped and destroyed. What remained of the 8th Army stumbled back chaotically into neighbouring Hungary. Bucharest, the capital of Romania, fell in short order on 31st August. Soviet forces swept on into neighbouring Bulgaria. Both countries surrendered. Without their Romanian allies, there was no way in which the Germans could continue to hold the Balkans.

D-DAY - WAR ON TWO FRONTS

On 6th June 1944, Josef Stalin finally got the second front he had always demanded. 156,000 American, British, Canadian and Commonwealth soldiers stormed the beaches of Normandy.

By the summer of 1944, the Nazis were being forced to fight on two fronts and divide their dwindling resources accordingly. Tanks and men, desperately needed on the Ostfront had to be sent west to meet the serious Allied challenge following D-Day in June. With threats to Army Groups North, Centre and South, the Germans were forced to gamble on where to place whatever resources they could muster.

ASSAULT ON THE FINNS

On 9th June, the Red Army unleashed a massive attack on Finnish positions on the Karelian Isthmus, desperate to avenge the humiliating war

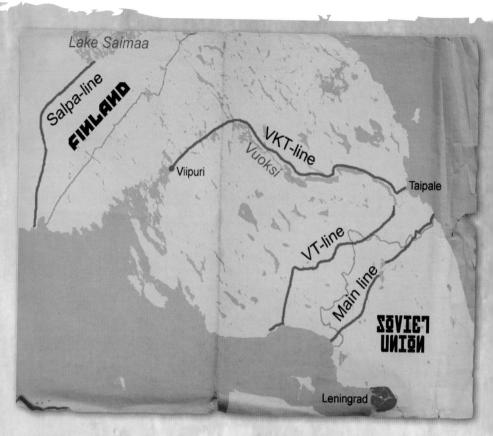

of 1940. Once more they failed. Three whole Armies of experienced troops were committed to breaking Finnish resistance. At first, they succeeded in breaching Finish defences in Valkeasaari on 10th June, forcing the Finns to retreat to the VT-Line, their second line of defence. Supported by swarms of bombers, tanks and artillery, the Soviets broke through this secondary line on 14th June and the Finns withdrew once more to the VKT-line. Here, they stood their ground more successfully and — after ferocious fighting in the battles of Tali-Ihantala and Ilomantsi, the Soviet offensive was finally halted. In September 1944, Finland quit the war and its soldiers now turned against their former German allies when they refused to leave Finnish territory.

OPERATION BAGRATION

On 22nd June (a day deliberately chosen because it was the anniversary of Operation Barbarossa), Soviet forces launched a ferocious attack on a seriously outnumbered Army Group Centre in Belorussia, supported by no less than 10,000 individual acts of sabotage and ambush by Partisan forces, principally on lines of German supply and communications. The operation had been preceded by a massive disinformation campaign and extensive use of camouflage. While it was impossible to completely hide 2.3

million troops as they manoeuvred into position, German intelligence did become deeply confused and their flawed reports helped to confuse Hitler too. He believed the Soviet attack would be against Army Group South in the Ukraine. He was wrong. He accepted their information over those of his commanders on the ground, who had a far better idea of what was really going on.

Based on this intelligence and therefore greatly underestimating both the numbers and the intent of the enemy, he told Army Group Centre to hold fast if attacked in key fortified towns — or Feste Platze. Hitler's generals begged him to change tactics but he refused. When the assault came — 4 entire Soviet armies against less than 800,000 German troops — the Feste Platze proved unable to stand up to the sheer weight and ferocity of the Soviet assaults and were besieged and then overwhelmed. Few Germans managed to break through the blockades and even fewer survived to return home to the west. By the time Bagration was over, Minsk had returned to Russian hands and 17 whole German divisions had simply ceased to exist. Another 50 divisions had seen their combat strength halved. Ten days after the recapture of Minsk, the Red Army had reached the pre-war Polish border with Germany, menacing East Prussia. Germany's response was to round up all available reserves in defence of the threat from the east. From now on, those waging war on the Western Front could not rely on receiving reserves of any significant size.

At the start of September, Germany had suffered 400,000 casualties. They'd also lost over 2,000 badly-needed panzers and 57,000 other motorised vehicles. The action had effectively seen the end of the German 4th and 9th Armies, as well as shattering losses to the 3rd Panzer Army in particular.

DAYS OF MIRACLES

As Bagration raged, Rommel and von Rundstedt went to Hitler and implored him to 'end the war'. Hitler was blunt and rude to them and rambled on about his new 'miracle weapons' that would yet win the war for Germany. Two days later, von Rundstedt was sacked as Commander in Chief West (Twelve days before that very meeting, one of those war-winning miracle weapons — the V-1 Flying Bomb — had accidentally flown off course on its way down to London and instead landed on top of Hitler's very own bunker.)

LVOV - SANDOMIERZ

The Soviets launched Operation Lvov—Sandomierz on 17th July 1944, sending the German forces left in Western Ukraine reeling back in shock. Lviv itself was liberated on 26th July. Elements of the Ukranian nationalist militia contributed to the liberation alongside the Soviets but it was soon made abundantly clear to them that Ukraine would now be under the boot of the Soviets. It would never enjoy independence.

CONFINED TO BED

In September 1944, Hitler suffered a nervous breakdown and was confined to bed. He was up and about again by November but seemed now to be totally incapable of reigning in his furious temper. Having survived a serious bomb plot by his own military back in July — and a further half dozen attempts to kill him back in 1943 — Hitler was starting

LEFT: Light field howitzer in firing position

MIDDLE: Hasso von Manteuffel with Colonel Niemack during Operation Bagration

RIGHT: Dynamite and ignition cables in preparation for blowing up railway tracks in Grodno

BELOW: Two Destroyed Panzer IV belonging to the 20. Panzer Division, Bobruisk

BOTTOM LEFT: Panzer IV

BOTTOM MIDDLE: Battle of Vilnius. Soviet and Polish Armija Krajowa Soldiers

BOTTOM RIGHT: Soviet soldiers in Polozk, Belarus

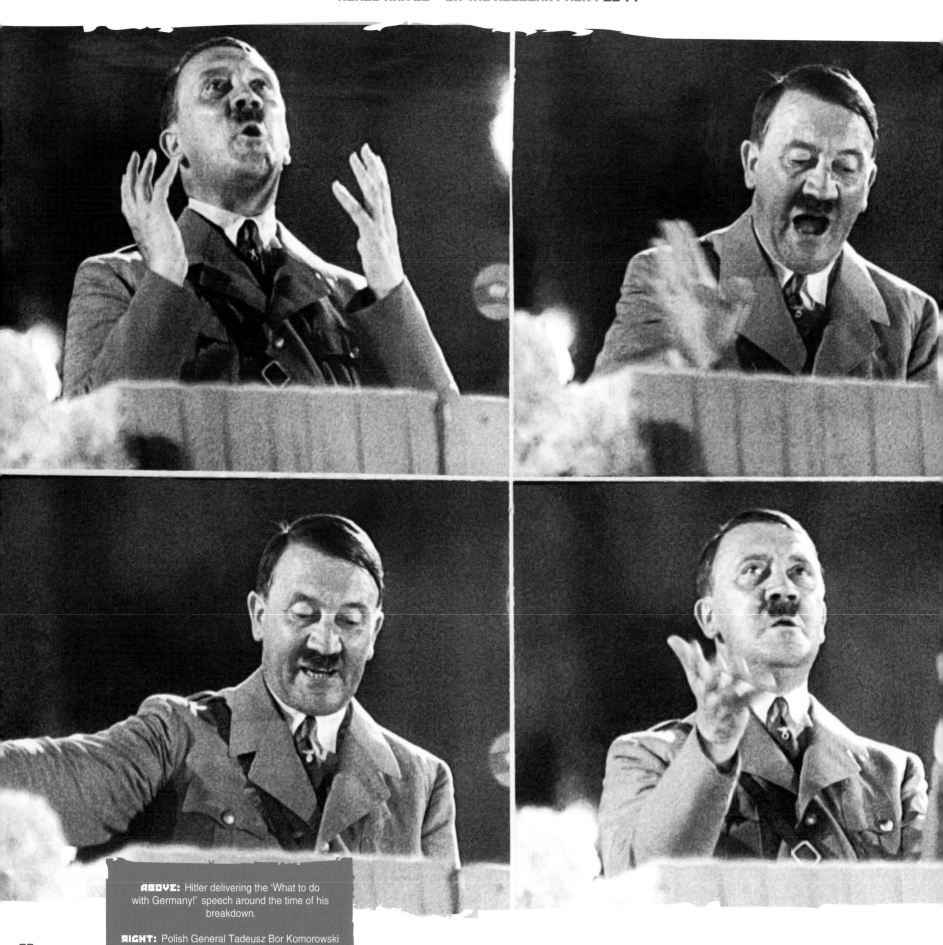

ABOVE: Hitler delivering the 'What to do with Germany!' speech around the time of his breakdown.

RIGHT: Polish General Tadeusz Bor Komorowski

to suspect that he wasn't as popular as he thought he was. Lying there under fresh sheets, he began to seethe with bitterness and hatred for the Germany he had once so loved.

LIBERATION

As Soviet forces swept west, they began to discover the ramshackle facilities holding Russian prisoners. For those who were liberated however, the danger was not yet over. Stalin had declared previously that there were no prisoners — only traitors to the motherland. Many faced interrogation by the secret police and faced charges of collaboration with the enemy. Women soldiers often fared the worst as they were widely accused of surviving only by whoring themselves to the Germans. Many prisoners were sent on to labour camps in Siberia. Others were killed on the spot.

THE WARSAW UPRISING

In August 1944, Stalin performed one of the most cynical, self-serving and murderous orders of his life. He encouraged the people of Warsaw to rise up against the Germans, promising them vital support. When 500,000 troops and civilians rose up together to fight their invaders under General Komorowski, Stalin immediately reneged on his promises and sat back and did nothing.

Other Allies including the British and Americans, as well as elements of the Free Polish Air Force, tried to supply the patriots from the air but could do very little in practicality. The Allies also tried to pressure Stalin into dropping supplies. He responded by giving the hard-pressed Poles an air supply drop comprising just 50 pistols and two machine guns. It was meant to be insulting. The fighting men of Warsaw, the men most capable of providing resistance to Stalin, were subsequently butchered by the Nazis.

There were units of Free Poles fighting alongside the Russians in the area at the time. They disobeyed the orders of their Soviet masters and did what they could to help, but were comprehensively beaten away by the German garrison in the city. Their leader, Lieutenant-Colonel Zygmunt Berling, was then stripped of his command by the Red Army.

How useful for Comrade Stalin to have his present enemies cut down the men and women who might have proved to be his future enemies, once Russia had replaced Germany as conquerors of Poland. The uprising lasted until early October during which time 300,000 Poles went to their deaths. The Germans revenged themselves by committing numerous atrocities on civilians and destroying large swathes of the city.

SLOVAKIA

On 8th September, Soviet forces engaged the Axis on the Slovak—Polish border, at a place called the Dukla Pass. It took two months for the Soviets to finally punch a whole into Slovakia, by which time they had lost close to 20,000 troops.

VOLKSGRENADIERS

By September, the shortage of German troops was so grave that Himmler and Goebbels set about putting together 25 divisions of Volksgrenadiers — units comprised basically of young boys from 15 to 18 years of age and old men from between fifty and sixty. They swore mighty oaths of loyalty to the Fatherland and to the Führer but the truth was somewhat more tawdry; if they deserted or otherwise ran away, their families would suffer. Greatly.

SLAVE LABOUR

Despite the sharp reverses in the war, in September 1944, the number of foreign slave labourers being abused within the German borders amounted to an incredible seven and a half million people working in mines, factories and fields. In 1942, Hitler had personally requested half million Slav women be shipped to Germany to act as domestic slaves

and thereby improve the lot of German housewives. Well over two million more people — POWs — were also being put to work as slaves. Many were worked to death or died of starvation or exposure. In one tiny example of cruelty, French slaves at one of Krupp's manufacturing plants were housed in dog kennels — with five men to each kennel. No water was provided. (The same company built a factory to exploit victims at Auschwitz.)

THE WAR FOR HUNGARY

The Red Army attacked Hungary in October 1944, but were badly beaten at Debrecen. For a while their advance stalled, but then they pushed on with renewed determination. By 29th December, Budapest was effectively encircled. Its 188,000 defenders would manage to hold out until mid-February 1945, by which time 38,000 of its civilian inhabitants had succumbed to starvation or enemy bombardment. German forces made three desperate attempts to break the siege of Budapest. Each attempt failed. The German Army was simply no longer strong enough. The Soviets celebrated taking the city by indulging in mass rape.

THE TRAPPING OF ARMY GROUP NORTH

Army Group North was cut off from other German forces by a Soviet manoeuvre that saw the Red Army reach the shores of the Baltic on 10th October. 250,000 men from Army Group Centre were now effectively pinned down on the Latvian Peninsula in what became known as 'The Courtland Pocket.' They would fight on until the end of the war.

ABOVE: Soldiers of the fourth Romanian army during an attack at Debrecen, Hungary

OPPOSITE PAGE
LEFT: Warsaw Uprising, German SdKfz 251 captured by Polish insurgent

MIDDLE: Warsaw Uprising, Roman Marchel "Rom" standing with German MP-40 in the region around barricade on Ciepla Street

RIGHT: Warsaw Uprising, Young Soldiers from the "Radoslaw Regiment"

A VISITOR FROM THE WEST

In October 1944, Winston Churchill travelled to Moscow to hold a bilateral meeting with Stalin. Nothing came of it. Stalin saw Churchill as increasingly irrelevant to the war. After he had gone, Stalin said with glee, *'We fucked this England!'*

ON THE GERMAN BORDER

With Germany in their sights, the Soviets now paused to regroup. They had advanced so far and so fast that they had gravely overextended their supply lines. The Germans ahead were defending their homelands now, which gave them powerful extra motivation to fight and with a shortened German line the enemy could concentrate his forces. Now the Soviets paused and instead started to build new roads and new railways, to bring massive amounts of supplies and ammunition up to the frontline. When the final assault came, they would want for nothing.

CHRISTMAS SPIRIT

Over Christmas and New Year, Guderian made no less than three separate attempts to stress the importance of building fresh defences in the east (Hitler had already announced at the time of the Ardennes Offensive in December 1944 that he thought a Soviet invasion of Germany in 1945 was a huge bluff). He tried to stress to the Führer that it was vital to keep Upper Silesia in particular because it was the centre of the German armaments industries. On the third visit, Hitler lost his temper completely. He started swiping out at the maps Guderian had prepared for them, screaming that they were *'completely idiotic'* and the man who made them should be locked in an asylum. Beyond caution now, Guderian started screaming back at the Führer.

'The Eastern Front is like a house of cards!' he bellowed. 'If the front is broken through at one point all the rest will collapse'.

AND THAT IS WHAT HAPPENED.

ABOVE: Ukrainian, Odessa residents welcome Red Army soldiers

1945

'The Germans are not human beings. From now on the word German means to use the most terrible oath. From now on the word German strikes us to the quick. We shall not speak any more. We shall not get excited. We shall kill. If you have not killed at least one German a day, you have wasted that day … If you cannot kill your German with a bullet, kill him with your bayonet. If there is calm on your part of the front, or if you are waiting for the fighting, kill a German in the meantime. If you leave a German alive, the German will hang a Russian and rape a Russian woman. If you kill one German, kill another -- there is nothing more amusing for us than a heap of German corpses. Do not count days, do not count kilometres. Count only the number of Germans killed by you. Kill the German -- that is your grandmother's request. Kill the German -- that is your child's prayer. Kill the German -- that is your motherland's loud request. Do not miss. Do not let through. Kill.

Soviet propagandist Ilya Ehrenburg

THE JANUARY OFFENSIVE

On 17th January 1945, the Soviets finally surged into Warsaw, inheriting a city comprehensively burned and pillaged by the retreating Germans. From here, the Red Army quickly went after the Nazi forces to the west across the Narew River. They enjoyed a huge numerical advantage — they had six times as many troops and tanks. The Germans had nothing that could stop them. Almost from the start, the Soviets were advancing at speeds of 40km a day. They seized the Baltic States, Danzig, East Prussia, Pozna☐ and then drew themselves up on a line to the East of the Oder river. They started crossing on 5th February. To the west lay the ultimate prize, Berlin, just 60 km away. Breslau was surrounded by 15th February and Poznan fell just a week later. In March, Soviet forces occupied Silesia precisely as Guderian had feared and paused — just temporarily — on the banks of the Neisse.

THE WAR IS LOST

On 30th January Albert Speer, the man in charge of German armament production, told Hitler in a memo that the war was now lost. The deciding factor had been, just as Guderian had predicted, the loss of Silesia with its vast coal mines and giant industrial

ABOVE: Soviet propaganda poster 'Death to German Fascist Invaders!' Artist K. Avvakumov

OPPOSITE PAGE: Ilya Ehrenburg

To 30 March   To 11 May

plants. It was all over. Hitler's response was to declare that he would never be alone in a room with Speer ever again, as he always seemed to bring bad news.

FIGHTS WITH GUDERIAN

By the end of January, Guderian tried to demand that the remains of Army Group North be evacuated by sea. Hitler in turn stood in front of him furiously brandishing his fists until Guderian's Chief of Staff yanked Guderian back by his uniform to stop him getting actually punched by the Führer. A fortnight later, Guderian went up against Hitler once more and in his diary, records a vivid picture of the man with whom he then had a two hour stand-up row…

'His fists raised, his cheeks flushed with rage, his whole body trembling, the man stood there in front of me, beside himself with fury and having lost all self-control. After each outburst Hitler would stride up and down the carpet edge, then suddenly stop immediately before me and hurl his next accusation in my face. He was almost screaming. His eyes seemed to pop out of his head and the veins stood out on his temples…'

DESPERATE DREAMS

On 25th January, Guderian was accused of high treason for suggesting an armistice in the west so that Germany might be allowed to devote its resources to fighting off the Russians. Barely two days later Hitler, Göring and Jodl were somehow convincing themselves that the Allies wouldn't even need to be asked for an armistice in the West. They would be begging Germany for it. After all, who wanted to see the Soviets win? Göring predicted a desperate and fawning telegram from England to that effect in just a bare few days. The gathering was, to all intense and purposes, a Mad Hatter's Tea Party in jackboots.

SALVATION FROM THE WEST

Hitler and other top Nazis were not the only ones to be looking to the West for salvation. Even before the Americans and British had crossed the Rhine, German soldiers were surrendering to them in droves. They were sick of war — and sick with fear of having to face the Russians on the Eastern Front. The Wehrmacht were wise to what was going on. Anyone found to be obtaining leave papers *'deceitfully'* or found to be in possession of false papers was to be executed it was announced in February 1945 — as would any German soldiers found wandering off from their units and claiming to be *'lost'*. German officers found to have failed to hold key objectives would also be executed. They started to run too.

ABOVE: Adolf Hitler talking to (L-R) General Guderian, Field Marshal Von Bock and Field Marshal Keitel

OPPOSITE PAGE: Albert Speer and Adolf Hitler discuss matters of war

YALTA

The Yalta Summit in February 1945 between Churchill, Stalin and Roosevelt only emphasised and confirmed Russia's growing power in the world. Roosevelt by this time was sick — indeed dying — and no match for Stalin's cunning or will. In Churchill's eyes, the Americans were now prepared to side with Stalin's communism over British imperialism. This was a truly disastrous policy shift, in the Prime Minister's eyes, but he simply could not get through now to Roosevelt in any meaningful way. President Roosevelt died of a massive stroke on 12th April 1945. His replacement, Harry Truman, was far less enamoured of Stalin (whom he referred to as '*a little squirt*') but by now much of the damage had been done.

SCORCHED EARTH IN GERMANY

On 19th March, Hitler issued a Führer Order which commanded the destruction of anything and everything within Germany which was likely to be of use to the enemy. Critics came to call it 'The Nero Order'. It was a military tactic but more than that, it was Hitler's last attempt to punish the German nation for letting him down and not being up to the task of destroying the sub-humans to the east. Any German who remained alive after the coming conflagration, he railed, would not be worthy of the splendour of Germany. Beside him, Martin Bormann ordered all Germans and slaves to go on a death march to the centre of the Reich, their mass starvation causing such chaos that it would end the war. Behind the scenes

Albert Speer worked desperately to stop it all being put into effect. Hitler's authority was rapidly crumbling alongside his dreams and his cities.

FATE IN THE STARS

In April, Hitler called for the horoscope he had had drawn up in 1933. It pointed out that the Führer would achieve a positive change of fortune in 1945, starting in April. Goebbels wasted no time in telling the German people that — according to astrology — they were now certain to win the war. Doubters doubted — and then the news came through that President Roosevelt had died. Goebbels and Hitler were elated. That was the change of fortune predicted by Hitler's horoscope. ..

RETAKING THE DANUBE

Increasingly losing touch with reality, the Führer ordered an-all out attempt to retake the river Danube. It failed, as the German forces available were just too weak and ill-equipped. After ten days of ferocious fighting, the Germans had made some progress but then were hit by such an overwhelming Soviet counterattack that everything they had gained was lost to them in a single day. The victorious Soviets flooded into Austria, Hitler's birthplace. Vienna fell on 13th April to the 3rd Ukrainian Front. A puppet government under Karl Renner was set up in short order and this announced that Austria had now left the Axis.

A BLOODY SIDESHOW

Five days earlier, the Soviets finally seized Konigsburg in East Prussia as surviving German forces retreated to the northernmost extremities of the land and continued to offer resistance until the end of the war. The fighting here was, it transpired, unimportant to the final outcome — but it provided one last bloody nose delivered to the Soviets. In what was later calculated to be one of the largest campaigns ever fought by the Soviets during the entire war, they came to lose well over half a million men and three and a half thousand tanks and artillery pieces in what was essentially a completely pointless fight. To any other country, that alone would have been a knock out blow. But Russia wasn't simply another country.

POISED ON THE ODER

By mid-April, the Soviet forces poised to strike from the East bank of the Oder were simply overwhelming in number. Encamped along the length of the river were some 2.5 million Russian soldiers, over 6,000 tanks, 41,000 artillery pieces, more than 3,000 Katyusha rocket launchers and 7,500 fighter aircraft and bombers. Berlin was now just 100 miles away. Germany braced itself. What else could it do?

ABOVE LEFT: Harry S Truman

ABOVE RIGHT: Martin Bormann

OPPOSITE PAGE: In the grounds of the Livadia Palace, Yalta during the eighth day of the Yalta Conference. Standing behind the three leaders are, L-R British Foreign Secretary, the Rt Hon Anthony Eden, MP, the American Secretary of State, Mr Edward Stettinius, the British Permanent Under-Secretary of State for Foreign Affairs, the Rt Hon Sir Alexander Cadogan, the Soviet Commissar for Foreign Affairs, Mr Vyacheslav Molotov, the American Ambassador in Moscow, Mr Averell Harriman

STALIN'S VISION

Back home, Josef Stalin checked his maps and indulged both his ambition and his paranoia. He had just conquered all of Eastern Europe — and he had no intention to ever let it go again. Thus he now saw himself as having two battle aims. The first was to conquer Berlin and deliver the final knockout blow to the Nazis. The second was to sweep westwards as hard and fast as possible to seize as much German territory as he could grab before the Americans and British got there. To keep his new Eastern Empire he was going to need a strong and deep buffer zone.

A third thought entered his mind. Zhukov and his other commanders were getting lots of credit for waging the war so well. This made them potential future leaders — and rivals to Stalin himself. He worked hard now to attach his own name to all the great victories while downplaying the achievements of his loyal commanders. In his mind he could already see them executed or exiled when war was done — filthy traitors that they undoubtedly were.

THE SEELOW HEIGHTS

Blocking the Soviet advance of Berlin now were German defensive positions up on the Seelow Heights. 90 metres high, 17 km back from the banks of the Oder River and 90 km east of Berlin itself, comprising anti-tank ditches, gun emplacements, bunkers and infantry trenches. Between the river and the heights, German engineers hastily took advantage of the natural flood plain — releasing the water from a nearby reservoir and turning the area into one filthy quagmire,

The Germans could muster just 100,000 men and 1200 panzers to hold the lines. The Soviets enjoyed a numerical advantage of 10 to 1. On 16th April, Soviet forces finally advanced West over the Rivers Oder and Neisse. The 1st Belorussian Front assaulted the Seelow Lines directly, backed up by massive artillery and aerial support. Meanwhile the 2nd Belorussian Front flanked them from the north and 1st Ukrainian Front outflanked them from the south. The Seelow Heights fell within just four days, costing the Soviet Union 33,000 casualties. 10,000 Germans were killed or wounded on the Heights. The way to Berlin was clear and open. In came the Russians…

RIGHT: An improvised dog-drawn cart brings a wounded soldier of the Red Army to a Soviet hospital station

ЯΛPΣ

'The little daughter's on the mattress /Dead. How many have been on it /A platoon, a company perhaps?'

Alexander Solzhenitsyn, Nobel Laureate

One of the horrifying distinguishing features of the final Soviet rampage through Germany was its sheer indulgence in atrocity — particularly in mass acts of rape. Apologists for these war crimes have said that the Soviets were just taking a natural revenge on those who had done such terrible things against the Soviet Union. Other historians point out that the advancing Russians were not particularly picky about the nationality of the women they raped along the way. They were simply men with guns who could force their own will onto the helpless. Antony Beever, an historian who wrote comprehensively of these atrocities, called them the, *'greatest phenomenon of mass rape in history'*, and said that it even made him reconsider the extreme feminist view that *'all men are rapists'* that he had once so vehemently disagreed with. Maybe men simply were vile after all and, given power, would naturally behave like depraved beasts.

Stalin was told about the horrors being unleashed against German civilian refugees by some of his more humane commanders but just shrugged and even chuckled a little. *'We lecture our soldiers too much,'* he said. *'Let them have some initiative'.*

Arch Soviet propagandist Ilya Ehrenburg simply exorted:
'Kill! Kill! In the German race there is nothing but evil. Stamp out the fascist beast once and for all in its lair! Use force and break the racial pride of these German women. Take them as your lawful booty. Kill! As you storm forward. Kill! You gallant soldiers of the Red Army.'

Of course, no records were kept of the number of rapes committed against German women and girls. Some serious and sober estimates put the number as high as two million. Age was no protection. 240,000 women are said to have died as a direct result. Many committed suicide. Many others killed their own children rather than let them fall into the hands of the Soviets.

It is believed that at least 100,000 women were raped by Soviet soldiers during the conquest of Berlin alone and its immediate aftermath. Some victims — survivors of their original ordeals — were then *'exported'* to Siberia for the use of men in labour camps there. Over half would die within just six months.

The raping of German women and children by their Soviet occupiers continued for as long as 1948, when Soviet authorities finally confined their troops to remote barracks specifically to stop them. Not because they cared, but to halt a tidal wave of STDs. Today, the Soviet War Memorial in Treptower Park, Berlin, is still referred to bitterly by older Germans as the *'Tomb of the Unknown Rapist.'*

German women and children were not the only victims. 100,000 women were believed to have been raped by Russian soldiers in Vienna alone, perhaps 50,000 in Budapest (including female embassy staff from neutral or friendly countries) and indeed women were abused in every single country the Russian Army swept into.

OPPOSITE PAGE: German girl raped by Polish marauders on the train home from Silesia is assisted from the Stettliner railroad station by fellow travellers

ABOVE: A German woman carrying a few possessions runs from burning buildings in Seigburg, Germany

SALVATION FROM THE WEST?

By now many German Generals whether in Berlin or scattered about a nation that had become one big battlefield, were fervently praying that the Americans would come and take the capital instead of the Russians. The Americans, at least, were civilised whereas the Russians had proven themselves rapacious beasts. This was never going to happen. The Supreme Commander (Western) Allied Expeditionary Force, General Eisenhower had never made any plans to take Berlin. It would obviously fall to the Soviets and there were great fears of numerous 'friendly fire' incidents should the two competing armies both surge into the city. The Russians could have them.

BERLIN - THE FINAL ASSAULT

Berlin was now within the Soviet's sights. The assault was to be jointly commanded by Marshals Zhukov and Konev — a deliberate move by Stalin so that no one man could get all the applause and credit back home. This resulted in a dreadful mess and confusion as the two men's armies effectively started to race each other and became entangled in each other's sectors of operation. Casualties were greatly increased and the pace of the victory slowed to a significant extent,

Commencing on 20th April — Hitler's birthday — Konev's 1st Ukrainian Front attacked the last scrappy remnants of what had once been Army Group Centre from the south while Zhukov's forces started shelling Berlin city centre. The bombardment would not cease until the city had surrendered. They fired more tonnes of high explosives into the city in two weeks than the Allied bomber formations had dropped on it in the whole of World War Two. That same night, Göring and Himmler both fled the city. By 24th April, Berlin was surrounded, with Russian units fighting their way through some of the outer suburbs. Less than a week later, Soviet forces were deep within the city fighting their way

ABOVE: Soviet bombers are engaged in military operations in the Battle of Berlin

OPPOSITE PAGE:
TOP LEFT: Soviet attack aircraft attack targets in Berlin

BOTTOM LEFT: Eisenhower and Churchill shooting the M1 Carbine during preparations for Operation Overlord

BOTTOM MIDDLE + RIGHT: German air defence on the rooftops of Berlin

through to the last holdouts of the Nazis as two million trapped civilians took what shelter they could. If any German household raised a white flag, the SS were under strict orders to shoot and kill all those inside.

THE BEAST CONSUMES ITSELF

Facing the Soviets in the streets of Berlin were 100,000 hastily conscripted 'soldiers' — mostly young boys hardly more than children and old men grandly termed the 'Volkssturmmann'. Untrained, vastly outnumbered and poorly equipped with whatever weapons could be scrounged up, they didn't have a prayer — and Soviet forces in the city now outnumbered the German defenders by more than 15 to one. Any little boys who refused to join up would be hung on the spot by the SS as an example. 'He who is not brave enough to fight has to die' was the stark message. Eyewitnesses described Berliners being strung up and hung everywhere — by their own soldiers and police. Men, women, children. If a tree wasn't available than a lamp post or street sign would do. There are stories too of mothers desperately searching the ruins, dodging bullets and shells to find their conscripted children and then take them home and hide them away, fully aware that their entire family would be executed by the SS were they to be caught.

HALBE

Hitler hoped desperately to save Berlin by teaming up the 70,000 troops of General Wenck's 12th Army positioned south west of the city with the remains of General Busse's 9th Army, who had come streaming back from defeat at the Oder river. They were then to unleash the counterattack of all counterattacks

against the Soviets threatening Berlin. In reality, neither general intended any such thing. They were going to move west as fast as humanly possible and surrender to the Americans before the Soviets got them. Many, after all, were SS and would be shown no mercy if captured by the Russians. The manoeuvre failed utterly. Konev's Soviet forces comprising some 280,000 men cut off the 9th Army in a forest close to Halbe, South Berlin and just annihilated it. Zhukov's men added to the slaughter by attacking German forces from the rear. Of the 150,000 men of the 9th, only around 30,000 broke through to link up with the 12th. So bad was the carnage that dozens and dozens of bodies still turn up in the area every year to this day.

HITLER - THE LAST DAYS

'Poor, poor Adolf. Deserted by everyone, betrayed by all'

Eva Braun

Hitler had retreated to his Führerbunker, located 55 feet under the Reich Chancellery building at the start of 1945, to better micromanage the defence of the Fatherland.

In between directing the war, Hitler enjoyed nothing more than launching himself into interminable monologues about everything from modern art, race and philosophy to dog training and advanced war-winning technology. In the bunker, his favoured topics narrowed further: dog training, the evils of smoking, suitable health foods and the rank stupidity of the average German plebian. Many of his Generals had long since turned to drink to deal with having to sit

LEFT: Soldier with woman explaining the handling of a bazooka, March 1945

MIDDLE: Volkssturm target practice, an officer explains how to use the weapon

RIGHT: General Ivan Konev

BELOW: 3 Volkssturm with their Bazookas at the ready

BOTTOM LEFT: Soldiers of the victorious Red Army celebrate in Berlin

BOTTOM MIDDLE: Berlin, German soldiers surrender of weapons

BOTTOM RIGHT: Soviet soldiers hosting the Soviet flag on the balcony of Hotel Adlon in Berlin

ABOVE: Russian soldiers Jegorow and Kantarija hoisting the Soviet Flag on the destroyed Reichstag building

OPPOSITE PAGE
LEFT: Adolf Hitler and Eva Braun at the Berghof

MIDDLE: Stars & Stripes newspaper announcing the death of Adolf Hitler

RIGHT: An American soldier poses next to an effigy of Hitler hanging in front of a barracks in the Buchenwald concentration camp. Grafitti on the side of a barracks reads "Hitler must die for Germany to live"

through them.

On 21st April he gave orders for SS-General Felix Steiner's Army Detachment Steiner to move to the rescue of beleaguered Berlin. When he discovered the next day that his orders had not been obeyed and the unit had not moved as ordered, Hitler started screaming, burst into tears and ended up in a state of total nervous collapse. As he recovered, he resumed screaming about how his incompetent generals had betrayed him and admitted — for the very first time — that Germany had lost the war. As his followers begged him to leave Berlin, he refused their requests. He would stay here and die, just to spite a Germany who did not deserve him.

That same day, 22nd April, Hitler went to see SS physician Dr. Werner Haase to ask him about the most reliable method of suicide. The good doctor recommended a combination of cyanide and a bullet to the head. When Göring heard about Hitler's suicide enquiry, he eagerly asked for permission to take over the Reich in what would be the Führer's rather long absence. Hitler took this the wrong way, accused Göring of planning a coup against him, threatened his arrest and mentioned something about execution. Within a day, Göring was under detention by the SS.

Communications had never been good in the Führerbunker. Someone had overlooked building a proper system. During the last days of Berlin, German intelligence officers were reduced to phoning members of the public (when phone lines were working) and asking them if their area was full of Russians yet, to get any measure of the Soviet advance. By 27th April, the Führerbunker had lost all communications. Everything was hearsay and rumour and scraps of paper in the hands of runners. When a story reached Hitler that Himmler was planning to negotiate a surrender with the Americans, he had one of his close associates (By chance, Eva Braun's brother-in-law) shot and ordered Himmler to be arrested for treason.

On 28th April, Hitler learned that his fellow fascist Benito Mussolini had been executed by partisans. This turned his thoughts to suicide once more. At a little after midnight, he married his mistress Eva Braun (who regularly referred to her beau as *'the Chief'*. He called her a *'country bumpkin'*). Joseph Goebbels and Martin Bormann were witnesses. The couple exchanged gold rings taken from victims killed by the Gestapo (Unfortunately both were too large) and celebrated with a small wedding breakfast. Within a few hours, Hitler was writing his last will and testament, blaming *'international Jewry'* for every single aspect of the war. During the day that followed, Hitler's mind turned more towards suicide — but he was dubious of the potency of the cyanide capsules he had been given and had them tested on his beloved German Shepherd Blondi. She died.

On 30th April, the Soviet Army was less than 500 metres from the Führerbunker. Hitler had a last meal of spaghetti with a raisin and cabbage salad, said his personal farewells and Hitler and Eva then retreated to his study. A gunshot was heard an hour later. On entering, Martin Bormann found Eva dead from cyanide and Hitler slumped forward in a chair with a bullet hole in his right temple. Eva had apparently refused to shoot herself as she wanted to look *'beautiful in death'*. Unhappily for her, the effect of ingesting cyanide greatly discoloured and distorted her face.

Their bodies were then taken up to into the Reich Chancellery garden outside the bunker alongside excited shouts of *'Hurry up upstairs they're burning the boss!'* In the garden, the two bodies were doused in petrol scavenged from abandoned cars and set alight while those few

present gathered round and gave a final Nazi salute against the backdrop of a thunderous Russian artillery bombardment. By all accounts the remains of Hitler and Eva did not burn very successfully and — after several attempts — what was left was bundled into a shallow grave in the early evening.

That evening Joseph and Magda Goebbels killed themselves too, along with their six children, each made to swallow cyanide in their sleep. Some of the remaining soldiers and staff then escaped the bunker. In those last desperate hours, it was every man and woman for themselves.

Winston Churchill made a brief visit to the Reich Chancellery on July 16th. He stood in the garden where Hitler and his wife had been buried, sneered, gave a quick V for victory sign and then left to do something else.

SURRENDER

Stalin knew within 13 hours that Hitler was dead. He never quite trusted the news and so kept an open mind. Perhaps the Führer had made a last minute ingenious escape, like in those cheap American movie serials. The news of Hitler's death was given to the German people via a radio station in Hamburg. They were told that Hitler has *'fallen at his command post, fighting to the last breath against Bolshevism and for Germany'*

The Mayor of Berlin made the official surrender of the city on 2nd May. Fighting continued until 8th May as some surviving German units battled their way west to surrender to the Americans or the British rather than the Russians. The fight for Berlin had resulted in 361,367 Russian casualties. No one knows how many Germans died. 500,000 is a conservative estimate. German forces beyond Berlin surrendered unconditionally on 7th May 1945, with German Chief-of-Staff General Alfred Jodl signing the order.

In the immediate aftermath, Zhukov signed three humane orders to help the people of Berlin, bringing food into the starving city, supplying quantities of milk for infants and trying to restore civil life to as near to normal as might be possible. He also issued orders to *'respect the German people'*. He got on well with the other Allied commanders, especially Eisenhower and — had Stalin not pulled him away within a year — history might have been very different.

ABOVE: Field Marshall Wilhelm Keitel signing the unconditional surrender of the German Wehrmacht at the Soviet headquarters in Karlshorst, Berlin

RIGHT: Victorious Russian soldiers in Berlin

ONCE MORE INTO THE BREACH

Was it all finally over? Winston Churchill had become so alarmed over the intentions of Stalin that he actually had plans drawn up to launch a secret surprise attack on the Red Army, starting on 1st July. The plan even involved fighting alongside rearmed German Army units against the Soviets. It was called Operation Unthinkable. His Chiefs of Staff Committee obviously agreed with the name — and successfully talked Churchill out of starting World War Three.

VICTORY

A victory parade was held in Moscow's Red Square on 24th June and Stalin allowed Zhukov to inspect the parade, riding on a white charger.

Within a year, Zhukov would be gone, purged on entirely trumped up charges that he was planning a coup. Stalin was merciful and sent him into exile deep in the Russian interior rather than killing him. When the hero of the Eastern Front was brought down, no one complained. No one dared. Uncle Joe also conducted yet another purge of his officer class — the men who had won the war for him. This time there were fewer firing squads and more humiliating demotions and obscure postings. Perhaps he was feeling almost grateful.

OR PERHAPS NOT.

ABOVE: Marshal Georgy Zhukov and Marshal Rokossovsky during the Victory Parade

RIGHT: Soviet propaganda poster. The slogan reads ' We Won!'. Artist V. Ivanov

9 мая 1945 г.
РАЗГРОМЛЕНА ГЕРМАНИЯ
ЗАВЕРШЕНА ВЕЛИКАЯ ОТЕЧЕСТВЕННАЯ ВОЙНА

СЛАВА НАШЕМУ

МЫ ОБЕДИЛИ!

3 сент. 1945 г.
ПОВЕРЖЕНА ЯПОНИЯ

ОКОНЧЕНА ВТОРАЯ МИРОВАЯ ВОЙНА

ВИКТОР ИВАНОВ-45

...ИКОМУ НАРОДУ, НАРОДУ-ПОБЕДИТЕЛЮ!
И. СТАЛИН.

AFTERWORD

BLOOD OMELETTES

The war between the armies of the Soviet Union and Nazi Germany and its Axis allies on the Eastern Front between 1941 and 1945 was nothing less than the largest military clash the earth has ever known. In scale, it resembles nothing else in human history. For four terrible years, frankly unimaginable numbers of soldiers and tanks fought across a battlefield more vast than can scarcely be imagined and at times more bitter and inhuman than can ever be endured.

It's estimated (everything in such utter carnage must be estimated) that over five million soldiers of the Third Reich and its allies died here. Eight out of every ten German soldiers who were killed during the war died here on the Eastern Front. The Soviets are said to have lost ten and a half million of their own soldiers — three million murdered while in German prison camps. Enormous figures. Staggering statistics — but simply as nothing when compared with the civilian deaths that occurred.

The war on the Eastern Front was a particularly evil war. To serve the purposes of Hitler's Third Reich, it was specifically intended — engineered even — to cause as much civilian loss of life as inhumanly possible. Hitler wanted to kill them. Stalin wanted to use them. Hitler wanted them gone. Stalin wanted them as a nice thick human shield between himself and the Nazis. Once Stalin had decided to fight to the very last man (woman and child), he employed his subjects to ensure that he would be that 'very last man'. How many Soviet civilians died? No one really knows. 25 million is a popular figure but the death toll keeps being revised upwards still by Russian historians. They died in their millions of shot and shell, but they died in still greater numbers of disease, hunger and exposure. They died in fire. They died of rape. They died of torture. They died clutching their babies in vans designed to smother them with carbon monoxide. They died in extermination camps. They died in every way it's possible to kill a helpless human being. The largest number of civilian deaths recorded in one single city was 1.2 million men, women and children during the Siege of Leningrad. Almost two thousand Soviet towns and cities were damaged or destroyed. Another 70,000 villages for the most part simply disappeared — plundered and burned for firewood or simply ploughed under the panzer tracks.

It's a great pity that Josef Stalin probably never said 'One death is a tragedy. One million is a statistic' as he is commonly believed to have done. At once, such thinking would have provided an invaluable insight into the creatures who command such wars whilst revealing that any statistic you read is worthless. A smokescreen. A husk sucked dry of all meaning and human experience. Millions upon millions upon millions died the most horrible deaths imaginable and yet could at the end of the day be neatly summed up in a few lines of some ledger.

'You can't make an omelette without breaking eggs' is probably the most vile and hateful proverb in the English language. It is an expression that could only be embraced by the very worst of humanity. It is an expression that defines human life as useful or worthwhile only if it serves the purposes of some sociopathic leader. Both Hitler and Stalin were keen on making omelettes. Hitler wanted a Brave New World like something out of a cheap Science Fiction Pulp. Stalin wanted a world where he stayed forever in charge — and bugger the politics and philosophy.

And the reality? Laurence Rees, in his excellent BBC book 'War of the Century' reminds us of a young girl who made omelettes to survive starvation in Kharkov in the winter of 1943 — omelettes made not of egg but of stale human blood fried in a pan. One girl. One story. One real horror. Statistics tell you nothing. Blood omelettes tell you everything.